THE **ROCKEFELLER** FILE

SECRET

R

by Gary Allen

'76 PRESS

Seal Beach, California

Other books by Gary Allen:
Communist Revolution In The Streets
Richard Nixon: The Man Behind The Mask
Nixon's Palace Guard
None Dare Call It Conspiracy

Published by
'76 Press
P.O. Box 2686
Seal Beach, Calif. 90740

Copyright © 1976 by Gary Allen

Print History

| January 1976 | 250,000 |
| February 1976 | 250,000 |

Library of Congress Catalog Card Number 75-39136
International Standard Book Number 0-89245-001-0

MANUFACTURED IN THE UNITED STATES OF AMERICA

Introduction

Dear Reader:

The super-rich in America enjoy power and prerogatives unimaginable to most of us. Who can conceive of owning a private empire that includes 100 homes, 2,500 servants, untold thousands of luxuries, and untold millions of dollars?

America has a royal family of finance that has known such riches for generations. It is, of course, the Rockefellers. But if the Rockefellers were content with their wealth, if their riches had satisfied their desires, this book would not have been written. And I would not be urging you to read it.

Money alone is not enough to quench the thirst and lusts of the super-rich. Instead, many of them use their vast wealth, and the influence such riches give them, to achieve even more power. Power of a magnitude never dreamed of by the tyrants and despots of earlier ages. Power on a world-wide scale. Power over people, not just products.

The Rockefeller File is not fiction. It is a compact, powerful and frightening presentation of what may be the most important story of our lifetime—the drive of the Rockefellers and their allies to create a one-world government, combining super-capitalism and Communism under the same tent, all under their control.

For more than one hundred years, since the days when John D. Rockefeller Sr. used every devious strategy he could devise to create a gigantic oil monopoly, enough books have been written about the Rockefellers to fill a library. I have read many of them. And to my knowledge, not one has dared reveal the most vital part of the Rockefeller story: that the Rockefellers and their allies have, for at least fifty years, been carefully following a plan to use their economic power to gain political control of first America, and then the rest of the world.

Do I mean conspiracy? Yes, I do. I am convinced there is such a plot, international in scope, generations old in planning, and incredibly evil in intent. You will find the truth—often surprising, sometimes unpleasant, always vital—in the pages that follow. Gary Allen has done a masterful job of combining the hundreds of scattered facts and hidden clues of the Rockefeller puzzle until one unmistakable pattern emerges.

The picture that is revealed when **The Rockefeller File** is finally opened may shock you. In this book, you will learn why the Rockefellers follow the policies they do, what their goals are, where they intend to take America . . . and why it is essential they be stopped.

I urge you to read **The Rockefeller File**—and to encourage your friends to do the same.

LAWRENCE P. McDONALD
Member of Congress

November 1975

Dedication:

To Floyd Paxton

Freedom never had a truer champion;
I never had a better friend.

Table of Contents

The Brothers Rockefeller, inheritors of a colossal fortune, are using their massive wealth, power, and prestige to create what they call the "New World Order." Shown above (from left to right) are David, Chairman of the Board of both the Council on Foreign Relations and the Chase Manhattan Bank; Winthrop (now deceased); John D. III, an advocate of people control; Nelson, the "political" Rockefeller; and Laurance. After years of planning and campaigning, a brilliant *coup d'etat* has finally installed Nelson (below) in the White House, without the risk of an election.

Chapter One
The Multi-Billion Dollar Myth

If you're thinking of colossal economic power, it doesn't exist. We have investments, but not control.

Nelson Rockefeller

At his Vice Presidential confirmation hearings, Nelson A. Rockefeller was as solemn and serious as P. T. Barnum swearing his freak show denizens were the real McCoy when he told the assembled solons:

I hope that the myth or misconception about the extent of the family's control over the economy of this country will be totally brought out and exposed and dissipated . . . There is not this network of control which is popularly conceived.

The Senators could not have been more polite. Nobody guffawed. The transcript does not indicate that they even tittered. After all, fools seldom get elected to the Senate these days. Nelson and David, as leaders of the Rockefeller Clan, are the nation's undisputed economic kings. No politician with enough savvy to be elected dog catcher laughs at a king.

Guessing the magnitude of the Rockefeller financial empire has been a favorite indoor sport since the turn of the century. In a front-page story on September 29, 1916, the *New York Times* reported that family patriarch John D. Rockefeller's oil holdings alone were worth $500 million, and that he was America's first billionaire. Eight hours after the story appeared his oil shares had increased in value by a tidy $8 million. Not a bad return for a single day's labor, even for a Rockefeller.

About this period, however, the picture of the family's growing financial might becomes more murky. The Rockefellers began hiding their wealth from the public—

and the tax collector—in trusts and foundations. As reported in the *Washington Post*:

> For two generations, the great fortune passed down by John D. has been fractionated and made more complex by increasing layers of trusts and closely held companies, where no public reports are required, none volunteered, and all inquiries politely rebuffed.

The Rockefellers invented a scheme, used by the super-rich today, whereby the more money you appear to give away, the richer and more powerful you become. Through the help of captive politicians, guided by some bright boys in the family law offices, legislation was written and passed which would protect the Rockefellers and other elite super-rich from the repressive taxation they have foisted on everyone else.

The key to this system is *giving up ownership but retaining control*. For example, most people don't believe they really own something unless they retain title to it in their own name. The Rockefellers know this is a big mistake. Often it is better to have your assets owned by a trust or a foundation—*which you control*—than to have them in your own name.

For example, when Judge Kenesaw Mountain Landis ordered Standard Oil broken up back in 1911, sly old John D. simply created some new foundations and gave his stock to them. The net effect was the same as if you took your wallet out of your right-hand pocket and put it in the left. In this case, however, Rockefeller not only managed to avoid income taxes, but also escaped the probate, estate and inheritance taxes which have ravaged the wealth of those not in the know.

So three generations of Rockefellers have been "giving away" millions of dollars—giving much of it to themselves. For example, if a Rockefeller gives a million dollars worth of stock in the Titanic Oil Corporation to the Dogood Foundation, which the family controls, he is not really out one million bucks. All he has done is transfer title of the securities to an *alter ego*. Of course, the foundation may then give away some of the money, or, more likely, donate some of the stock's future earnings to some allegedly worthwhile cause. But, as the few investigations by Congress into this devious field have shown, in the case of the Rockefellers such bequests somehow end up increasing the Rockefeller financial or political power.

The upshot is that, through the past six decades, the public has had no way even to estimate Rockefeller wealth, let alone accurately measure the family's power and influence. But we can make some logical extrapolations from the few facts that are available. We know that through the magic of compound interest (as they say down at your friendly savings and loan branch), one dollar invested at the modest rate of five percent per annum will double in thirteen years. This means that if the Rockefellers were earning only five percent per year (a return they would find laughable), that modest $1 billion fortune in 1916 would have grown to over $22 billion today.

The late Stewart Alsop, a reporter who had excellent sources in the Eastern Liberal Establishment (a euphemism for the financial, political, academic and media mafia controlled by the Rockefellers), used to scoff at the usually accepted *Fortune* magazine estimate of the family's fortune at between $1 and $2 billion.

"It would not be at all surprising," Alsop concluded in his book *Nixon And Rockefeller* (published in 1960), "if all the Rockefeller family assets—all the Rockefeller-controlled money as well as the Rockefeller-owned money—came to something like 10 billion dollars."

If Alsop is correct, the Rockefeller holdings would now be a rather comfortable nest egg of some $25 billion.

In view of the fact that the past fifteen years have produced much economic growth (as well as much inflation), it could well be that $25 billion is a reasonable, even a conservative figure.

Of course the family has never admitted being worth even a sizeable fraction of this amount. When originally queried by the Senate Committee, good ol' Nelson estimated his personal fortune at a paltry $33 million. After some very mild prodding by the Committee, this modest estimate was increased by 660 percent.

The Vice Presidential hopeful eventually admitted to being worth a more respectable $218 million—a sum, incidentally, that is greater than the *combined* wealth of all 37 Presidents in this country's history.

So great was public suspicion of the Rockefeller wealth that the family's financial adviser, J. Richardson Dilworth, was invited to testify before the House Judiciary Committee. Dilworth became the Rockefeller family's key money manipulator in 1958. Prior to joining the Rockefellers he had been a partner in Kuhn, Loeb & Co., perhaps the most politically powerful international banking firm in the world. Kuhn, Loeb was, and still may be, a satellite of the immensely rich and powerful Rothschild family of Europe. Historically, the Kuhn, Loeb name has been synonymous with financial success and political intrigue, dating back to participation through senior partner Jacob Schiff in bankrolling the Bolshevik revolution in Russia.*

In the past, the Rockefellers have both competed with and cooperated with the Rothschilds. Dilworth's leaving Kuhn, Loeb & Co. to take control of the Rockefeller family purse strings was considered *very* significant by students of the international financial and political machinations of the super-rich.

Dilworth maintains an office designated as Rockefeller Family and Associates, occupying three entire floors at 30 Rockefeller Plaza. Rockefeller Family and Associates is not a legal entity or corporation; it is simply a name to describe the organization which coordinates and manages the investments of the 84 descendents of John D. Rockefeller, Jr.

With the well-oiled assurance of a successful mortician, the urbane, sophisticated Dilworth laid to rest the com-

---

*This story is told in detail in the author's book, *None Dare Call It Conspiracy*. See order blank in the back of this book.

mittee's concern over the family's financial muscle. He used five charts, crammed with statistics, to dispel the notion that the family exercises inordinate power over the nation's economy. Rocky's critics found it difficult to dispute Dilworth's bewildering collection of figures; at times they could hardly keep up with them. The whole performance was as confusing as an Eisenhower press conference, and probably as deliberate. As one observer commented:

> . . . the talk of convertible stocks, coupons and fiduciary obligations and the fact the vast holdings of The Rockefeller Foundation and other family-collected funds were not included in Dilworth's presentation left most members little more enlightened than they had been.

According to Dilworth, the 84 living Rockefellers are worth a mere $1,033,988,000. (Presumably he rounded off the figures to the nearest thousand dollars.) The bulk of the assets disclosed by Dilworth were held in two trusts, one established by John D. Jr. in 1934 for his children and one set up in 1952 for his grandchildren.

But according to many sources, the Rockefellers have as many as 200 trusts and foundations, and it is possible they have hundreds, even thousands more. Why bother with so many? For one very simple reason: So that assets can be moved, merged, and manipulated so smoothly and so quickly that the public—and just as important, the tax experts from the Treasury Department—have no way of knowing just how much money is where.

Suppose you had three buckets, one empty, two filled with water. Is there any way you could pour water from one bucket to another so quickly an observer could not tell how much water you had?

But suppose, instead, you had five thousand buckets. And a hundred persons to help pour. And you were allowed to keep all but a few buckets and a few pourers hidden behind a high wall. Would your chances be better to keep your "liquid assets" secret? So it is with the Rockefellers. All trusts are not equal. Only a handful of attorneys in the country know how to establish the type of trusts the Rockefellers have. These specialized trusts are most emphatically *not* the sort your friendly local solicitor can create for you. They not only can eliminate probate, cut inheritance taxes, and reduce income taxes; unlike corporations, they can achieve almost total privacy. Theoretically, trustees can, within the privacy of their directors' meetings, create more and more trusts *ad infinitum*. With a little effort, taxes disappear. With more effort, even the value of the holdings can be completely hidden.

This explains why the Rockefellers use so many trusts. The fact is that we really don't know how many trusts the family has established. It may be thousands, or tens of thousands. Remember Nelson's explanation for the embarrassing fact that he did not pay any income tax in 1970—his trust fund managers had done a lot of shifting of investments in 1969. You can bet they moved their assets to accomplish this!

In testifying before the Judiciary Committee, Dilworth did not discuss the family's holdings by individuals, but presented them as a single package. Dilworth said he had received "unanimous permission" from the Rockefeller family to make public the total figures of their holdings. "This in itself has been a unique experience, since it runs so completely against the grain of what we in the office consider to be one of our major responsibilities—the preservation of the separate identity and highly personal treatment of each account," he said. "Like other Americans, they value highly their right of personal privacy."

More importantly, the privacy within the trusts can conceal whatever assets the Rockefellers decided not to make public. If the family had chosen to open up the minutes of its trustees' meetings to Congressional investigators, we might have some idea of the true financial status of the family. No such suggestion was even whispered. We really have only the Rockefellers' word for the amount of wealth they control, and they obviously have a vested interest in minimizing its size.

How about assets hidden in foreign countries? Are there

Swiss bank accounts? Rocky says no, but he could be telling the literal truth, yet have foreign accounts held by trusts or other nominees, or securities "in street name" (that is, in the name of a brokerage firm such as Merrill Lynch). Or assets can be held in a custodial account of a bank, such as (for example) Chase Manhattan.

All that we know for sure is the first time Rocky was asked about his wealth he swore it was a paltry $33 million; later he admitted the figure was six times higher. A slight miscalculation which anyone might make.

We are supposed to swallow the propaganda that the Rockefellers are merely middle-class millionaires, not even in the same financial ball park as Howard Hughes or those Texas wheeler-dealers. But, "Hideout Howard" and the Dallas money crowd are relative Johnny-Come-Latelys to the world of high finance. The Rockefellers have been refining oil for over a century and running banks for 75 years. Although it cannot be proven because the evidence is hidden, few sophisticates swallow Dilworth's $1 billion figure—which does not even include any personal residential property, jewelry or other personal belongings; nor does it include Nelson's art collection, which he has valued (conservatively, we must assume) at $35 million.

Nor are the Rockefeller homesteads your basic tract bungalows. The main homes of the clan are located at Pocantico Hills in New York. Established 45 years ago by old John D., the land alone was worth $50 million in 1930. Their value today defies estimate. When opened to the press for the first time in 1959, at the time of the marriage of Nelson's son Steven, the estate, with its 70 miles of private roads, was said to be 4,180 acres in size. Earlier reports claimed 7,500 acres. In 1929 there were 75 buildings occupied by the Rockefellers and their attendants; over 100 families lived on the estate. One addition has been a $4.5 million underground archives to store family records. One wag has described the palatial Pocantico Hills as the kind of place God would have built if he had had the money.

No expense was spared by the family to remove minor

blemishes on their pastoral paradise. The senior Rockefeller gave the New York Central Railroad $700,000 to move its tracks, and $1.5 million to a small college to shove off.

Among the other chateaus owned by Nelson is the enormous Monte Sacro Ranch in Venezuela, his coffee plantation in Ecuador (the one where Juan Valdez waits for the perfect day to pick the beans), his several farms in Brazil, his 32-room Fifth Avenue duplex in New York City, the mansion in Washington, D. C., the little hideaway at Seal Harbor, Maine, etc., etc., etc.*

In addition, at last count the Rockefellers owned seven huge ranches. Earlier this year [1975], Nelson bought 18,000 empty Texas acres for "outdoor recreation."

It is doubtful if any of the Rockefeller women will ever have to spend the night at the YWCA. The four of them have about 100 residences to choose from, including John D. III's spacious Beekman Place apartment in Manhattan, Laurance's sumptuous resorts in Hawaii and Puerto Rico, Nelson's Venezuela Finca, (large enough to swallow the entire city of New York), and David's Caribbean home.

Needless to say, it takes an army of underlings to operate these elegant pads. There are 500 full-time domestics, gardeners, guards and chauffeurs at Pocantico Hills alone, 45 at the family's Seal Harbor, Maine, retreat, and 15 in Nelson's Fifth Avenue apartment. All told, it has been estimated the Rockefeller women have at their beck and call about 2,500 servants.

Because the Rockefellers are forever on the wing—in their private jet fleets—each residence is permanently staffed, and nightly the sheets are turned down. One never knows when the boss might pop in.

Of the corporate holdings described by Dilworth, the largest, of course, is Exxon, the new name for Standard Oil of New Jersey, one of the companies formed when John D. Rockefeller, Sr. was ordered to de-monopolize the

---

*The Congressional hearings revealed that two houses in Washington—ostensibly owned by a Rockefeller attorney — actually belong to Nelson.

Standard Oil Company. The stock directly owned by the family (not counting that held by such family-controlled entities as banks and foundations) amounts to $156.7 million. Number two on Dilworth's list is Rockefeller Center, which the canny money manipulator valued at a mere $98 million. Anyone who accepts this estimate of the Center's worth is probably negotiating to swap his lifetime savings for sole proprietorship in the Brooklyn Bridge. The *Los Angeles Times* observed on September 30, 1974:

> Nobody but the stockholders (the four surviving Rockefeller brothers—Nelson, John D. III, David and Laurance—their sister, Abby, and the heirs of their brother Winthrop, who died in 1973, and a handful of Wall Street bankers) know its true value, but the educated guess of New York's real estate crowd is that Rockefeller Center, land and buildings, is worth $1 billion.

Next in line in the family portfolio is $85-million worth of stock in Standard of California, followed by $72.6 million worth of IBM. Companies in which the family holds $10 million or more in stock include Chase Manhattan Bank, Mobil Oil Corp., Eastman Kodak, General Electric, Texas Instruments, and Minnesota Mining and Manufacturing. Altogether the Rockefellers own a significant portion of some 50 major American companies.

So extensive are the family's holdings in securities that the Dilworth operation spreads over three entire floors at Rockefeller Center, and requires 154 full-time employees to manage the security portfolios. Working under Dilworth's supervision are fifteen top financial experts, who also double and triple in brass by serving on the boards of directors of nearly 100 corporations with combined assets of some $70 billion.

When testifying before the Judiciary Committee, Dilworth's main objective was to fortify Nelson's statement that his family's reputed financial power was a "myth" concocted by evildoers. "If you're thinking of colossal economic power, it doesn't exist. We have investments, but not control," claimed Rocky.

"It should be stressed that both the family members and their investment advisers are totally uninterested in controlling anything," parroted Dilworth. "The family members are simply investors. The aim and hope of the advisers is over time to achieve a reasonable total return for our clients." So seriously was the whole performance taken that not even a wink could be detected in the hearing room, much less a discreet nudge under the table.

Dilworth maintained that members of the family do not coordinate their investments. Their sharply differing views on investments, social and environmental policies, Dilworth claimed, have prevented them from ever voting their stock in unison. "There is no grand design or overall pattern," the Rockefeller hireling assured the committee.

Dilworth went on to say that the last time the family interfered in the management of a company was in 1928, when John D. Sr. and Jr. forced Standard Oil Company (Indiana) to remove a chief executive. Such intervention now, purred Dilworth, is "totally foreign to this family. In the 17 years I've been on this job, I've never seen this family try to push people around."

The Wall Street Journal sprang to the defense of the family on September 25, 1974:

> . . . while Mr. Rockefeller is a bit modest about his economic clout, it is true that there are no individuals left in this society who are wealthy enough to alone substantially influence economic events. The wealth accumulated by John D. and the other tycoons of his era is diffused through a vast economy, controlled by foundations, trusts and the managers of large broadly based corporations. Power is diffused along with it.

In April 1958, when it was reported that J. Richardson Dilworth, the man with the most snobbish-sounding name since Junius Pierpont Morgan or Jackie Gleason's immortal Reginald van Gleason, was appointed to his present position, the *New York Times* explained that the organization "manages and supervises" the Rockefeller family investments. The phrase "manages and supervises" suggests a coordinated effort at directing family finances. If the Rockefellers were not interested in max-imizing their economic leverage, it would seem logical that each would pursue his own interests separately and retain his or her own battery of experts.

Dilworth makes it sound as if the family has widely divergent views on social, economic and political questions. Yet we have not been able to find a single significant occasion when the four sons and daughter of John D. Rockefeller, Jr. differed.*

And is it not curious that no member of the Judiciary Committee chose to grill Mr. Dilworth about the alleged disagreements which prevent the family from acting in financial unison? The *New Yorker* of January 16, 1965, tells us that the brothers and sister Abby "get together two or three times a year to discuss matters of interest to all of them." The purpose of the conferences is to "collide and coalesce," as one of their senior advisers described it.

Charles B. Smith, a top Dilworth lieutenant, was a bit more forthright than his boss: "Our goal, like everybody else's, is to make wads and wads of money for the Rockefeller family." The Rockefeller family likes money. But, once you have achieved the ultimate of opulence in your standard of living (and the Rockefellers reached that plateau decades ago), making money for its own sake becomes a fairly academic exercise.

Most people relax after they have reached the point of economic comfort and security. But, for some individuals, the ultimate ego trip has been the pursuit of power. In bygone days the rare individual with a manic desire for power seized a throne, or led conquering armies. Now that is all passé. Today, more worlds are conquered in board rooms than on battle fields. And, as we shall see, what happens on battle fields is often the result of decisions made in board rooms.

All of us can name plenty of tyrants and despots from

---

*One subject on which the family is unanimous is furthering Nelson's political ambitions; the Rockefellers have contributed a staggering $25 million to various campaigns promoting Nelson for the Presidency.

the past. Genghis Khan, Alexander the Great, Napoleon, Hitler, Stalin—these men brought misery and death to millions of people in the course of realizing their own perverted ambitions. But because the overwhelming majority of people do not possess such a psychotic thirst for power, they find it all but impossible to recognize its presence in others.

Most Americans just want to provide decent lives and comfortable futures for themselves and their families. They are willing to work hard to achieve the necessities of life and even many luxuries. But they could no more conceive of scheming, plotting and conniving to become economic commissars or kings than they would be interested in abandoning civilization for life as headhunters along the Amazon.

It is Mr. Average American and his family, however, who pay the price for the megalomania of the empire builders. Especially since our domestic would-be tyrants learned long ago that a political-economic conspiracy can become far more powerful than a criminal one—and is far, far safer for the participants.

Whether or not such megalomania is carried by genes, we do not know. What can be shown is that it has existed for at least three generations in the Rockefeller family. Despite the protests of the Rockefellers and their hirelings that they are totally uninterested in controlling anything, a survey of the evidence will reveal an all-consuming passion for control over everything and everybody.

The House of Rockefeller is not just a wealthy and successful family. Instead, it is an Empire. No other family has deliberately sought control over so many institutions— institutions which affect every facet of American life. Whether it is government, business, energy, banking, the media, religion or education, at the apex of the power structure you will find Rockefeller money and Rockefeller front men and agents. Such total pervasiveness, influencing every important aspect of American life, cannot be happenstance.

Chapter Two
The Saintly Sinner

Competition is a sin.

John D. Rockefeller

Enough books have been written to fill a fair-sized library, detailing the incredible story of how Daddy Oilbucks started Standard Oil and built the Rockefeller fortune. Some of them even tell the truth! We will tiptoe through these shady tulips only long enough to understand the traits and tactics of the Rockefeller founding father, so we may recognize them as they bloom again in modern clan members.

Everything about the Rockefellers seems to be controversial, even their family background. One story goes that the family descends from French Protestants, who changed their name from Roquefeuille to Rockefeller when they were driven from France into Germany. However, a genealogy compiled by the distinguished scholar, Dr. Malcolm Stern, entitled *Americans of Jewish Descent*, convincingly established the claims of many American Jews that the Rockefeller clan originally was one of their own.*

The controversy about the Rockefeller antecedents is probably not important. But it does highlight an accomplishment more difficult than threading a needle after six martinis (and one that is reported about as often).

The family controls oil holdings worth hundreds of millions in Arab lands, yet Nelson has remained the darling of organized Jewry in New York City. Without such support he could never have been elected Governor of

*Birmingham, Stephen, *The Grandees: America's Sephardic Elite*, Harper & Row, N.Y., 1971, p. 3.

New York State four times. Just how the family manages this bit of wizardry boggles the mind.

William Rockefeller, the father of John D., first became involved in the petroleum business when he peddled the oily stuff at $25 a pint as a cure for warts, snake bite, cancer and impotency. The wandering medicine man called himself "Doctor," even though he couldn't have entered medical school with a search warrant. In addition to being a quack, "Doc" Bill was a bigamist, horsethief and child molester. The good "Doctor" avoided prosecution in New York for raping a 15-year old girl by high-tailing it for Cleveland. Once there, he deserted his wife and six children to marry a 20-year old. (At least when Nelson abandoned his wife of 31 years to marry Happy Fitler Murphy, he did not abandon his children. She abandoned hers.)

Although no one ever nominated him for the father-of-the-year award, the "Doc" did take the time to instruct his children in his own unique business ethics. Author William Hoffman reports: "The thing the children most remembered about their father was the delight he took in getting the better of them in business deals. He would con them out of something they considered important, then lecture them on the necessity of always being alert."

The family's friendly biographer, Professor Allan Nevins, quotes "Old Bill" as boasting to a crony:

> I cheat my boys every chance I get. I want to make 'em sharp. I trade with the boys and skin 'em and I just beat 'em every time I can. I want to make 'em sharp.

He did.

The sharpest of the "Doc's" progeny was John D. Any psychiatrist worth a couch would trade several neuroses to have had a chance to learn what made him tick. He was full of more contradictions and paradoxes than a Charlie Chan flick. The main feature of his Jekyll-Hyde personality is that he was straighter than an arrow in his private life and deeply (some say fanatically) religious. At the same time he was totally and utterly ruthless in his grasping for money and power. Many of the old boy's victims were sure that his religion was a pretense, an act. But actually there is no evidence that his claims to piety were deliberately faked.

Unlike his father, John D. was a nose-to-the-grindstone type who, before he was out of his teens, was a shrewd and successful commission broker in Cleveland. In 1859, his partners sent him over to Titusville, Pennsylvania to see if there was as much financial potential in the gushing black liquid as was rumored. Young Rockefeller liked what he saw. He decided that of the three phases of the burgeoning oil industry—production, transportation and refining—the last promised the greatest profits.

John D. returned to Cleveland and launched what became the mighty Standard Oil Company. From the start of his business career, one thing that Rockefeller hated more than sin was competition. For John D., the only *efficient* way to run anything was by a monopoly. Provided, of course, that the most qualified, most capable, and most deserving person—meaning himself—ran it.

When John D. founded Standard Oil, it was just one of the 27 other refineries in the Cleveland area, and by no means the biggest. But the ambitious businessman—who once declared that "competition is a sin"—soon devised a plan to take on or destroy his competitors. The simplicity, audacity, and ruthlessness of his scheme is breathtaking.

He bribed and coerced the railroads serving the oil-producing region (the Pennsylvania, Erie, and New York Central), to give him a kickback, or rebate, not only on his own shipments, but also on every barrel his competitors sent by rail. The more they shipped, the more he made!

Rockefeller's rebate formula enabled him to reduce his own prices and drive the other oil refiners out of business *using their own money*! Within a year, his competitors had capitulated.

Lewis Corey, in his book *The House of Morgan*, comments on the ploys that provided the *coups de grace* to Rockefeller's competitors:

> . . . the battle of competition . . . was waged by means of

intrigues, discriminatory railroad rates, business blackmail and expropriating competitors' property . . . .

In spite of public condemnation, Standard Oil persisted
in extorting discriminatory rates from railroads, afterward
secured by John D. Rockefeller becoming a power himself
in the railroads, particularly New York Central, Erie and
Pennsylvania. Rate discrimination was general and
infuriated small businessmen to revolt . . .

John D. did not get his bag of tricks from his daily
reading of Matthew, Mark, Luke and John. The rebate
game was powerful, but it was only one of his cunning
schemes. In the early days, "lucky" competitors were
offered cash or stock in Standard Oil, in return for selling
their firms to Rockefeller at the rock-bottom prices he
offered. The smart ones took stock. Later, things got
rougher. Matthew Josephson describes in *The Robber
Barons* what happened to one stubbornly independent
company:

   . . . . where the Standard Oil could not carry on its expansion by peaceful means, it was ready with violence; its
   faithful servants knew even how to apply the modern
   weapon of dynamite. In Buffalo, the Vacuum Oil Co., one
   of the "dummy" creatures of the Standard Oil system,
   became disturbed one day by the advent of a vigorous
   competitor who built a sizeable refinery and located it
   favorably upon the waterfront. The offices of Vacuum
   conducted at first a furtive campaign of intimidation. Then
   emboldened or more desperate, they approached the chief
   mechanic of the enemy refinery, holding whispered conferences with him in a rowboat on Lake Erie. He was asked
   to "do something." He was urged to "go back to Buffalo
   and construct the machinery so it would bust up . . . or
   smash up, to fix the pipes and stills so they cannot make a
   good oil . . . And then if you would give them a little scare,
   they not knowing anything about the business. You know
   how . . ." In return the foreman would have a life annuity
   which he might enjoy in another part of the country. So in
   due time a small explosion took place in the independent
   plant.

Ferdinand Lundberg, in his study *The Rich and The*

Super-Rich, has observed: "As the history of Standard Oil by any author, pro or con, clearly shows, Rockefeller was of a deeply conspiratorial, scheming nature, always planning years ahead with a clarity of vision that went far beyond anything any of his associates had to offer."

John D. specialized in operating through others, just as the family does today. He hired agents everywhere; among competitors, politicians and in the media. He found plenty of people who could be bought. "The ability to deal with people is as purchasable a commodity as sugar or coffee . . . . I pay more for that ability than for any under the sun," the Standard Oil founder once admitted. Rockefeller's industrial espionage system was by far the most elaborate, most sophisticated and most successful that had ever been established. William Manchester tells us in *Rockefeller Family Portrait*:

> The trouble with fighting John D. was that you never knew where he was. He ran his company as though it were a branch of the C.I.A. All important messages were in code—Baltimore was "Droplet," Philadelphia "Drugget," refiners were "Douters," the Standard itself "Doxy." Shadowy men came and went by his front door, shadowy companies used his back door as a mailing address. For a long time the public didn't realize how powerful he was because he kept insisting he was battling firms that he secretly owned outright. His real rivals were forever discovering that their most trusted officers were in his pocket. The tentacles of the octopus were everywhere.

One Cleveland oil refiner made a last ditch effort to save his company from a Rockefeller takeover by going to Peru for oil. He found it had all been bought by a company which was a subsidiary of a corporation owned by the Anglo-American Company of England—which belonged to Standard. Soon, his firm was just another satellite in the Rockefeller oil empire.

It was not for nothing that newly impoverished former competitors referred to the Standard Oil biggie as John D. Reckafellow. A lot of bitter, broken men would have liked to have had a piece of that Rock.

In later years the Wizard of Oil tried to disguise his piratical business operations with the protective coloration of his religious practices. "God gave me my money," he piously proclaimed. Many wryly mused that if true, God had a very strange code of ethics.

By 1890, Standard was refining 90 percent of all crude oil in the United States and its world-wide operations were expanding rapidly. Many have been led to believe that the federal government finally broke up Standard's near monopoly. The truth is that when oil was discovered in Louisiana, Oklahoma and California, Standard Oil, big as it was, was unable to seize complete control of the mushrooming oil business. In the big oil boom that followed, too many small producers and refiners prospered for John D. to bribe, blackmail, or bomb all of them. In a sense, it was God, not Uncle Sam, who blocked John D.'s monopolistic plans.

Chapter Three
The Family That Preys Together

> *If Nelson Rockefeller becomes Vice President or events make him President someday, he will bump into his family's wealth on practically every major public issue . . .*

> Thomas O'Toole
> *Washington Post*

Although international banking is probably the Rockefellers' most important business, Standard Oil remains the keystone in the arch of the Rockefeller Empire. The family is still better known to the public for its oil properties than for its bank shares.

Petroleum is now the single most important commodity in world trade. It supplies the fuel, of course, for almost every motor vehicle in the world, it powers most electric generating plants, and it is the most vital raw material for the manufacturing of plastics, chemicals and drugs. All of this has brought huge benefits to the Rockefellers. As *Time* magazine reported in its issue of February 18, 1974:

> For 111 years, the business that has been variously known as the Standard Oil Trust, Standard Oil Co. (New Jersey), Esso and now Exxon has survived wars, expropriations, brutalizing competition, muckraking attacks and even dismemberment by the U.S. Supreme Court (in 1911). It has not only survived but has also grown—from a refinery in Cleveland to a global behemoth that sells petroleum in more than 100 countries through some 300 subsidiaries and affiliates that make up a "United Nations of oil." Not only grown but also prospered—so much so that last month it reported the largest annual profit ever earned by any industrial company: $2.4 billion after taxes.

The explosive growth of Exxon, the tiger of the oil industry, is revealed in the following UPI release fifteen months after the *Time* article:

> *Fortune* magazine has just issued its list of the nation's 500 biggest corporations, and never in the 20 years that it has tracked their performance have the rankings been so changed. The reason, the May issue of the magazine reports, is oil.
>
> *Fortune's* new list of the biggest publicly held industrial corporations for 1974 introduces a new No. 1: the Exxon Corporation. It displaced the General Motors Corporation, which had been America's biggest industrial company for 40 years. Exxon was No. 2 in 1973.
>
> Propelled by soaring prices for oil, Exxon's sales—the gauge by which *Fortune* determines size—surged from $25.7 billion in 1973 to $35.8 billion last year.

To get some idea of the mammoth size of Exxon, consider the following: If Exxon were shorn of all its foreign operations, it would still be the ninth or tenth largest industry in the United States. Yet it gets only 16% of its oil production and 32% of its sales from this country. If Exxon merely transported oil, it would be the world's biggest shipping firm. It has 155 tankers of its own and varying numbers under charter at sea. It is a substantial international banker, holding fortunes in marks, yen, francs, pounds and dollars all over the world. And on and on it goes.

In order to determine actual Rockefeller family control over Exxon and the other offshoots of the original Standard Oil Trust (Mobil, Standard of Indiana, Standard of California, Chevron, Sohio, Phillips 66, Marathon, *et al*), we must gather all of the pieces of the puzzle we can find and carefully fit them together. In his testimony before Congress, Dilworth revealed that the Rockefeller family has approximately $324,600,000 worth of oil stock. This represents an average of about 2 percent in each of the four giant oil companies. But, in 1966, testimony before the Patman Committee indicated that the nine Rockefeller family foundations also controlled an average of about 3 percent in the Standard Oil Trust descendants. This known total of 5 percent would give the Rockefellers effective working control over the four giant corporations.

In addition, there are shares held in trust by the Rockefeller banks, insurance companies, universities and other groups whose boards of directors and trustees are interlocked with the Rockefellers.

And yet, incredibly, oil is not even the Rockefellers' biggest business. That honor is reserved for international banking. The Rockefeller family banks are the First National City Bank and the Chase Manhattan Bank. The Chase Manhattan is the third largest banking establishment in the world; and while only number three, it is by far the most influential.

The largest bank in the world is Bank of America in California, inventor of the bank credit card, Bank-Americard, which now has 39 million cardholders worldwide. Bank of America became a giant through branch banking in California, where it has over 1,000 offices. Until recently, however, when it linked its overseas operations with the Rothschilds of Europe, the Bank of America lacked international horsepower. Now it too has joined the internationalists' crusade for World Government.

Chase Manhattan was created by the union of the Rockefeller-owned Chase Bank with the Kuhn, Loeb-controlled Manhattan Bank. The marriage has been a huge success for both families; in 1971 Chase Manhattan claimed $36 billion in assets. This is impressive enough, but the *New York Times* has pointed out that it is not the whole story: ". . . a major portion of their [Chase Manhattan's] business carried on through affiliated banks overseas is not consolidated on the balance sheet."

Time also emphasizes the immense power of the Chase Manhattan, noting that "The Chase has 28 foreign branches of its own, but more important, it has a globe-encircling string of 50,000 correspondent banking offices." Fifty thousand correspondent banks around the world! If each correspondent bank were worth only a paltry $10 million, it would give Chase potential worldwide clout of five hundred billion dollars! Such a figure is simply incomprehensible. Unfortunately, it is probably a conservative estimate of Chase's power and influence.

Such financial clout would give the Rockefellers the ability to create an international monetary crisis overnight. Could it be that it is they who have been yo-yoing the price of gold, dollars and foreign currencies during the past few years—creating panics for most investors, but profits for themselves?

Every time an international monetary storm blows up, hundreds of millions of dollars flow into European banks. When the storm subsides, those who were "in the know" at the beginning have made enormous sums of money. That the Rockefellers have been very profitably involved, through the Chase Manhattan Bank and its overseas facilities, seems more than reasonable.

By almost any standard, Chase Manhattan has become virtually a sovereign state. Except it has more money than most. It even employs a full-time envoy to the United Nations.

As just one illuminating statistic, during 1973 Chase board chairman David Rockefeller met with 27 heads of state, including the rulers of Russia and Red China, plus scores of lesser dignitaries. Not even Henry Kissinger, he of the "shuttle diplomacy" and much-publicized state dinners, can match Rockefeller's influence with the men at the top.

Chase Manhattan's annual reports contain much information detailing the worldwide expansion of the bank. It has gone international on the grand scale. And it shows no signs of slowing down. In fact, Chase Manhattan is the undisputed world heavyweight champion when it comes to international banking.

During the Senate hearing on Nelson's confirmation, he claimed, "I do not own any shares in the Chase Manhattan Bank." However, he neglected to mention that his family owns 623,000 shares, or 2.54 percent of the Chase Manhattan stock. And he also conveniently overlooked the fact that the Rockefeller Brothers Fund owns another

148,000 Chase shares and Rockefeller University holds 81,296.

Myer Kutz tells us in the *New York Times* of April 28, 1974: "The Rockefellers and Rockefeller institutions own a major, essentially controlling interest, estimated at more than 4%, in The Chase Manhattan Bank."

The Chase *Annual Report* for 1974 reports that the total assets of The Chase Manhattan Corporation stood at $42,532,003,302. That's over forty-two billion dollars. From this, reports Chase, they had a net income of $180,801,382 for the year 1974. That's over $180 million profit in just one year—or $3.5 million in profit a week—of which the Rockefeller family pockets over four percent, or roughly 7.2 million dollars. That's not bad, considering Chase is mainly a device for holding and boosting many of the family's other financial interests.

Once again we must note that actual ownership by the family in Chase Manhattan may be much greater than is admitted. Professor James Knowles in his highly detailed study, "The Rockefeller Financial Group," states:

> It is impossible to establish conclusively that the wealthy families represented on the boards of the banks in the Rockefeller Group own a controlling share of the stock. The ownership of large banks is a carefully guarded secret. Even when banks are required to disclose their largest stockholders, as was the case in the 1962 Patman investigation of chain banking, they have used what are called "street names" in referring to stockholding in trust. These "street names" are wholly fictitious and bear no resemblance to the actual beneficiary or trustees. In the case of Chase Manhattan Bank, for example, its reported twenty largest stockholders in 1962 included fifteen "street names," (e.g., Dudd & Co., Don & Co., Atwell & Co.) . . . .*

If fifteen of the twenty largest blocs of stocks are held in fictitious names designed to hide the identities of the real owners, it is impossible to doubt that some, if not most, of the actual owners are part of the Rockefeller Empire.

---

*Knowles, James, "The Rockefeller Financial Group," MSS Modular Publications, NY, 1973, p. 8.

When the few facts that are available to the public are considered—that the Rockefellers control by far the largest amount of stock in Chase Manhattan, that other families closely connected with the Standard Oil fortune from its beginning also own substantial blocks of stock, that the board of directors of Chase Manhattan reads like a who's who of Rockefeller lieutenants, and that David Rockefeller is chairman of the board of the bank—no one can dispute Rockefeller control of the Chase Manhattan Bank.

But Chase Manhattan is not the only mega-bank in the Rockefeller financial empire. The first bank with which the Rockefeller family became directly involved was the National City Bank of New York, which actually ranks number two in the international standings. Its former president, James Stillman, became a close associate of John D.'s brother, William, who was at the time managing the huge Standard Oil Trust. William Rockefeller tilted the Standard Oil banking business in Stillman's direction and thus National City became the largest bank in New York City. The financial marriage was cemented by the marriage of two of William Rockefeller's sons to two of Stillman's daughters.

Until his retirement in 1967, James Stillman Rockefeller, a product of the Stillman-Rockefeller merger, was chairman of the board of First National City Bank. Previously, James had strengthened the Rockefeller family and financial ties by marrying Nancy Carnegie of the fabulously wealthy Carnegie family.

City Bank has enjoyed such phenomenal growth that it now surpasses the mighty Chase in total assets. While it does not have the prestige or political muscle of the Chase, it really matters very little since both are Rockefeller family banks.

Yet a third large New York bank in the Rockefeller orbit is the Chemical Bank, which is controlled by the Harkness family. Edward Harkness was one of John D.'s closest business associates in the Standard Oil Trust, and as late as 1939 the Harkness family was the largest non-Rockefeller owner of Standard Oil stock.

Closely related to the Rockebanks are the gigantic insurance companies, with their investment funds worth hundreds of millions of dollars. Life insurance companies play a critical role in financing because they are the principal suppliers of long-term credit, whereas banks are mainly involved with short-term and medium-term credit. In turn the solvency (or bankruptcy) of other corporations is often dependent on their ability to obtain loans from the Rockefeller-controlled financial giants.

The Rockefeller Group of banks is heavily interlocked with the board of directors of three of the four biggest life insurance companies: Metropolitan Life, Equitable Life and New York Life. The total assets of these three insurance giants amounted to over $113 billion in 1969. According to Professor Knowles, the Rockefeller Group-controlled banks account for about 25 percent of all the assets of the fifty largest commercial banks in the country and for about 30 percent of all the assets of the fifty largest life insurance companies.

Buddy, can you spare a dime?

The Rockefeller family control over these banks and insurance companies gives them *leverage* over the economy that goes far beyond their direct ownership.

There are several ways in which the Rockefeller Clan controls vast segments of the economy. The first is through the stockholding of the families in the group. Five percent ownership of a widely held public corporation, according to a 1974 report by the Senate Banking Committee, is considered tantamount to control, especially if your name is Rockefeller. But if we consider only those firms where the Rockefellers own twice that much stock, or have five percent of the stock plus two or more top-level management positions, we can put the following companies in the column controlled by the Rockefellers. (The 1975 asset-size rating by *Fortune* magazine is indicated in parenthesis.)

Exxon (1), Mobil Oil (5), Standard of California (6), Standard of Indiana (13), International Harvester (26), Inland Steel (78), Marathon Oil (60), Quaker Oats (163),

Wheeling-Pittsburgh Steel (194), Freeport Sulphur, and International Basic Economy Corporation.

Another means by which the Rockefeller Group has potential influence or control over major segments of the economy is through the trust departments of the Rockebanks. Nearly a decade ago, the assets of commercial bank trust departments were $253 billion, almost $100 billion more than those of all mutual savings banks and savings and loan companies. Usually a commercial bank trust department exercises sole voting rights over the stock it holds. But anyone who believes this is the case for the enormously large trusts established for the Rockefeller family probably also hopes to find a real diamond in the bottom of his Cracker Jacks box.

While Dilworth was bending over backwards trying to convince the assembled Senators at the hearings that the family never, but *never*, interferes with management, *Fortune* magazine has reported that the Rockebanks often throw their weight into proxy battles, and the very knowledgeable Professor Knowles adds, "No company is secure from possible domination by bank trust departments."

In 1967, the Rockebanks had a total of $35 billion in trust department assets—nearly 14 percent of the national total! These included $22.5 billion in stocks. Knowles notes:

> Obviously, such stockholdings, most of which are either under the direct control of the families whose representatives sit on the boards of these [Rockefeller] banks or are indirectly under their control through voting rights exercised by the bank trust departments, provide a basis for the effective control of a large share of the American economy.

Chase's trust department, with the bank's companion investment management corporation, controls the *single* largest block of stock in 21 major American corporations. This means that United Air Lines, Northwest Airlines, Long Island Lighting, Atlantic Richfield Oil, National Airlines and 16 other multimillion dollar firms are also under the Rockefeller thumb.

The *Los Angeles Times* reports:

> Control of the bank and of its trust department has the effect of multiplying the family's economic leverage. Every major bank in New York holds millions of shares in trust for other owners—most of whom give the banks the power to vote the shares and, thus influence corporate management.

Corporations which are probably under the control of the Rockefellers, through financial institutions, trust departments or foundation ownership of stock, include the following (with the 1975 *Fortune* rating in parenthesis):

> IBM (9), Mobil (5), Texaco (4), IT&T (10), Westinghouse (19), Boeing (39), International Paper (56), Minnesota Mining & Manufacturing (59), Sperry Rand (70), Xerox (41), National Cash Register (97), National Steel (64), American Home Products (92), Pfizer (130), Avon (159), and Merck (152).

But wait, there's more! Still wonder if the Rockefellers have amassed a dangerous amount of power? Consider that just the transportation companies under Rockefeller influence (with 1975 *Fortune* ranking for transportation corporations noted in parenthesis) are as follows:

> Penn Central (T3), TWA (T1), Eastern Airlines (T8), United Airlines (T2), National Airlines (T26), Delta (T13), Braniff (T19), Northwest Airlines (T18), and Consolidated Freightways (T17).

Other major corporations in which the Rockefellers have significant influence, either direct or indirect, but not enough to prove working control, are:

> AT&T (U1), Motorola (149), Safeway (R-2), Honeywell (68), General Foods (58), Hewlett-Packard (225), and Burlington Industries (86).

Yet another manner in which the Rockefellers can exert significant control over corporations is through loans.

More and more in recent years companies have had to finance modernization and expansion through bank borrowing. Old John D., biographer Allan Nevins tells us, "never allowed any finance capitalist to obtain large shares" of his properties. While Big Daddy did not want to be eaten by the Wall Street loan sharks, he didn't mind becoming one. Roughly 80 percent of Chase's loan portfolio, the U.S.'s largest, represents major nationwide corporations. Bank of America, the nation's largest, specializes in making installment loans to millions of individual customers. The Rockefeller banks make fewer loans, but they make them to the giants of industry. According to Professor Knowles, the Rockefeller Group's position in the capital market is even greater than its share of banking and insurance assets would indicate. When a bank makes a large loan to a company, it is in a position to demand that it have a voice in the decision-making machinery of that company. Often this comes in the form of having somebody appointed to the borrower's board of directors.

This relates to yet another method for economic control, interlocking directorates. An interlocking directorate exists between two companies when a member of the board of directors of one company also sits on the board of directors of the other company. This was theoretically outlawed by Section 8 of the Clayton Act, which says that no person shall be a director at one time in any two or more competing companies. This law is enforced almost as strictly as the one against jaywalking in New York City. Tracing all of the interlocks among the Rockefeller Group's representatives on various boards of directors is a challenge that would reduce an Einstein to a babbling idiot. Just a few of the major corporations not previously mentioned that have interlocking-directorate ties with the Rockefeller Groups include:

Allied (Chemical) (85), Anaconda Copper (118), DuPont (17), Monsanto (43), Olin Mathison (161), Borden (47), National Distillers (185), Shell (14), Gulf (7), Union Oil (34), Dow (27), Celanese (101), Pittsburgh Plate Glass

(113), Cities Service (61), Stauffer Chemical (233), Continental Oil (16), Union Carbide (22), American Cyanamid (107), American Motors (93), Bendix (77), Chrysler (11), C.I.T. Financial (F9), S. S. Kresge (R5), and R. H. Macy (R27).

In case you were not able to keep a running total of all the firms enmeshed in the various strands of the Rockefeller web, let us summarize the *known* results: 37 of the nation's top 100 industrials, 9 of the top 20 transportation firms, the nation's number one utility, 3 of the 4 largest insurance companies, plus scores of smaller companies engaged in manufacturing, distribution, retail sales, loans, or investments, are controlled by the Rockefellers.

Staggering, isn't it? Put it all together and it does not spell M O T H E R. It spells P O W E R.

"The power of the family fortune is beyond measure," the *Washington Post* has reported. And this time the paper was telling the truth. "[It is] a nexus of ownership and leverage that is greater than the sum of its parts." But, says Rocky, it's all a myth! Sure, Rocky. And Raquel Welch is skinny, and Mark Spitz can't swim.

One or two Doubting Thomases have even wondered about whether it might be a conflict of interest to merge all of this monetary muscle with the political power of the Vice Presidency, and potentially the Presidency.

Wealth should not be an obstacle to high office, of course, providing that government stays out of business and business stays out of government. But, it is obvious that business and government have been getting closer and cozier for many decades. Today it is virtually impossible to tell who is seducing whom. Those on the ideological Left call it Corporate Fascism and those on the right call it State Socialism. *Both* are correct.

The point is that the Rockefeller family interests are so closely intertwined with matters of public policy, both foreign and domestic, that virtually every major governmental decision in some way affects the Rockefeller Empire. As Thomas O'Toole observes in the *Washington Post* (a paper that strongly supported Rocky's confirmation as Vice President):

If Nelson Rockefeller becomes Vice President or events make him President someday, he will bump into his family's wealth on practically every major public issue. . . .

Taxes, the environment, government regulation of business, prices, interest rates, overseas diplomacy, war and peace — Rockefeller interests are enhanced or hurt by government policy-making in practically every major area of American life. . . .

. . . . As Vice President or President, he couldn't very well disqualify himself every time a policy decision potentially affected Chase Manhattan Bank. He would be out of work if he did. Even if Rockefeller took a vow of poverty, this empire would remain intact, still dominated by his family.

But the Rockefeller wealth goes beyond this conflict-of-interest question.

What would a middle-level bureaucrat do, for instance, if he knew he was regulating the President's family fortune? Would a senator or congressman be able to resist the combined might of the White House and Wall Street's second-largest bank, not to mention all the corporations which do business there?

Rocky buried the entire issue, as far as Congress was concerned, when he asked: "Am I the kind of man who would use his wealth improperly in public office?" He knew that the question would satisfy the politicos on Capitol Hill, many of whom have received campaign donations from the Rockefeller Empire. Not one member of the Judiciary Committee had the nerve to answer his rhetorical question with the resounding "Yes!" it so richly deserved.

As we shall see, the Rockefeller family wants more money and more power. It will use its private fortune, its public position, and anything else it can to acquire it. The senior Rockefeller was a master Machiavellian who began by scheming against local competitors and wound up scheming with cartelists for economic control of the world. His heirs make his ploys look like the friendly bargaining of a Saturday afternoon garage sale.

Chapter Four
Profit Times Philanthropy Equals Power

Philanthropy is the essential element in the making of Rockefeller power. It gives the Rockefellers a priceless reputation as public benefactors which the public values so highly that power over public affairs is placed in the Rockefellers' hands. Philanthropy generates more power than wealth alone can provide.

> Myer Kutz
> *Rockefeller Power*

The foundation ploy was one of the cleverest moves shrewd old John D. ever made—and he was responsible for some lulus. By the turn of the century the tactics he had used to create the Standard Oil monopoly made his name synonymous with ruthless exploitation. He was known as John D. Reckafellow, with a worse reputation than Scrooge. He may have been the most hated man in America.

In order to scrub up his image (and possibly assuage his alleged conscience), John D. hired Ivy Lee, the nation's most prestigious ad man of the day. Lee suggested that the aging gentleman offset his skinflint image by starting to give away money. Scrooge was to be turned into an instant Santa Claus. To begin with, Lee (the original Madison Avenue truth-twister) had Mr. Standard Oily carry around a pocketful of dimes which he would strew before deliriously happy and grateful kiddies whenever he made one of his infrequent public appearances. Cynics observed that St. John ripped off money by the millions and doled it back a dime at a time.

Well, not quite. He had an even more Machiavellian scheme in mind. He would "give" money away to foundations under his control and then have those foundations spend the money in ways which brought even more power and profits to the Rockefeller Empire. The money "given" away would be bread cast upon the waters. But bread that almost always had a hook in it. John D. Jr. was to refer to this as the "principle of scientific giving."

The original Rockefeller foundation was established in 1901 and was called The Rockefeller Institute for Medical Research. It was set up as part of Lee's PR program to clean up the Rockefeller image. Doubtless the Rockefeller money has done much good in the field of public health and scientific research—although there are some who will give you a heated argument even here.*

By 1910, state after state was approving the 16th Amendment, which provided for a graduated income tax. John D. read the handwriting on the Congressional wall and, using his "deeply conspiratorial nature," began making plans to avoid the consequences of the tax by hiding his wealth in the Rockefeller Foundation.

One quite naturally assumes that the graduated income-tax, the second plank of the *Communist Manifesto*, would be opposed by the wealthy. The fact is that many of the wealthiest Americans supported it. At first the taxes were to be very small, and some of the super-rich may have promoted them out of altruism. But others backed the scheme because they already had a plan for permanently avoiding both the income-tax *and* the subsequent inheritance tax. John D. had figured out how to turn the lemon of the graduated income tax into lemonade for the House of Rockefeller. It is the most classic case of what accountants call "pre-tax planning" on record.

---

*Those who believe that Rockefeller "philanthropy" even in the health field is phony, point out the fact that Rockefeller monies have been used to degrade natural prevention of sickness and disease through vitamins and health foods and promote the use of drugs. Drugs are manufactured mainly from coal tar derivitives and, besides being in the oil business, the family has for decades been heavily invested in the giant drug manufacturing concerns. For more information on Rockefeller control of medicine, see G. Edward Griffin's World Without Cancer, Chapter XVI, Part II of a two-volume set.

The best way for the Rockefeller-Morgan *Insiders* to eliminate growing competition was to impose a progressive income tax on their competitors while making sure the law contained built-in escape hatches for themselves. Actually, very few of the proponents of the graduated income tax realized they were playing into the hands of those they were seeking to control. As Ferdinand Lundberg notes in *The Rich And The Super-Rich*:

> What it [the income tax] became, finally, was a siphon gradually inserted into the pocketbooks of the general public. Imposed to popular huzzas as a class tax, the income tax was gradually turned into a mass tax in a juijitsu turnaround . . . .

The *Insiders'* principal mouthpiece in the Senate during this period was Nelson Aldrich of Rhode Island, the maternal grandfather of Nelson Aldrich Rockefeller. Lundberg says that "when Aldrich spoke, newsmen understood that although the words were his, the dramatic line was surely approved by 'Big John' [D. Rockefeller] . . . ." In earlier years Aldrich had denounced the income tax as "communist and socialistic," but in 1909 he pulled a dramatic and stunning reversal. *The American Biographical Dictionary* comments:

> Just when the opposition had become formidable he (Aldrich) took the wind out of its sails by bringing forward, with the support of the President (Taft) a proposed amendment to the Constitution empowering Congress to lay income taxes.

The escape hatch was ready. By the time the Amendment had been approved by the states, the Rockefeller Foundation was in full operation. The careful orchestration of both parts of the campaign represents one of the most successful financial coups in history. The money the Rockefellers have made by it is incalculable. By exempting themselves from the burden they forced on their competitors, the Rockefellers were able to operate in a world of near *laissez-faire* capitalism while foisting the weight of more and more socialism on their competitors. It is the equivalent of a sprinter forcing every other runner in a race to carry a sixteen-pound shot.

Backing the graduated income tax had another timely advantage for old John. It was about the same time that Judge Kenesaw Landis was ordering the breakup of the Standard Oil monopoly. Wily John D. was able to kill several flying feathered creatures with a single hard object. He not only avoided taxes by creating four great tax-exempt foundations; he used them as repositories for his "divested" interests in the various Standard Oil entities. In the switch, Rockefeller had made his assets non-taxable so that they might be passed down through generations without being ravaged by the estate and gift taxes which everyone else had to pay. As Lundberg observed, old John D. planned ahead.

Each year the Rockefellers can dump up to half their incomes into their pet foundations and deduct the "donations" from their income tax. Nelson admitted at the confirmation hearings: ". . . the foundation pays no capital gains tax and no income tax so those funds can continue to multiply." They not only can, they do.

Having the foundations as a tax-free piggybank is only one of the advantages they provide the family. As *Business Week* has observed: "The real motive behind most private foundations is keeping control of wealth." In the foundation world, where "not-for profit" really means "not-for-taxation," one exchanges ownership for control.

The Rockefellers have further advantages with their foundations. They can buy, sell or hold real estate, stocks and other securities. Congressman Wright Patman, chairman of the House Banking Committee, has charged that the Rockefellers and other foundations act in concert, using their enormous portfolios to perform maneuvers which used to be known indelicately as "rigging the market."

So powerful have the major foundations become that the Patman Committee concluded: "Unquestionably, the economic life of our Nation has become so intertwined with foundations that unless something is done about it they will hold a dominant position in every phase of American life."

Since this report was issued by the Patman Committee in the early 1950s, absolutely nothing has been done about the power of the Rockefeller-controlled foundations — except to assist them to become even more powerful. And as this knowledgable study warned over twenty years ago, these foundations now do hold "a dominant position in every phase of American life," as we shall see.

It is the Rockefeller family which sits comfortably astride this foundation colossus. Collectively, the Rockefeller foundations have in excess of $1.5 billion in assets, but they also have interlocking control over the other most powerful foundations, the Carnegie Group and the giant Ford Foundation.

When you hear "Carnegie Foundation" think Rockefeller. For many years the five Carnegie foundations have been mere appendages of the Rockefeller octopus. The chief operators of the Carnegie foundations have for decades been members of the Rockefeller coordinating committee, the Council on Foreign Relations, the glue which holds the Rockefeller Establishment together. (The Council on Foreign Relations, or CFR, is the subject of the next chapter.) In addition, two of the six men on the Carnegie Corporation's finance committee are also directors of Rockefeller financial institutions.

The baby giant of the foundation world is the $3-billion-in-assets Ford Foundation. From 1953 to 1965, John J. McCloy was chairman of the Ford Foundation, during most of which time he was also chairman of the Chase Manhattan Bank. McCloy was succeeded by another Rockefeller minion, Eugene Black, a director of Chase Manhattan and former head of the World Bank. Currently running the show at the Ford Foundation is McGeorge Bundy, formerly on the payroll of the Rockefellers' Council on Foreign Relations. As with the Carnegie foundations, most of the trustees of the Ford Foundation are members of the Rockefellers' Council on Foreign Relations.

It is not too hard to see how, as the Patman Committee has charged, these foundations can collude to act as a single entity.

The terrible part of this business is that the economic fraud permitted the Rockefellers through their foundations—though maddening to the middle-class tax-payers who are aware of it—is the *least* malignant part of the foundation picture. It is the political and social impact of these foundations which is devastating. So serious is the matter, in fact, that even the irascible Congressman Patman has not dared venture into such affairs, knowing that the trail is littered with the bleached bones of imprudent Congressional investigators who sought to reveal how the Rockefellers are using the foundations in their grab for complete domination of the United States.

The first of the Congressional Committees to attempt such an investigation was the Cox Committee, created in 1952 under the leadership of Congressman Eugene E. Cox, a Democrat from Georgia. Warren Weaver notes in *U. S. Philanthropic Foundations* that the official purpose of this Committee was to determine which "foundations and organizations are using their resources for purposes other than the purposes for which they were established, and especially to determine which such foundations and organizations are using their resources for un-American and subversive activities or for purposes not in the interest or tradition of the United States."

"Liberal" Democrats in control of Congress first delayed the appropriation of funds for the Cox Committee, then gave it only six months to conclude an investigation that would properly require several years. Cox hoped to expose foundation fraud and the subversives behind it; but, as Dwight MacDonald has pointed out, "the strategy misfired, because the Democratic leaders, who were still in control of the House, boxed the impeccably Americanistic chairman with less dedicated colleagues." It was all-out war—with billions involved. The first battle ended with a serious casualty. Congressman Cox fell gravely ill during the investigation and died. Without his leadership, the Committee Report became a whitewash.

One member of that Committee refused to be a party to the coverup. He was Congressman Carroll Reece of Tennessee, a former Chairman of the Republican National Committee and one of Robert Taft's campaign managers. Reece promptly demanded a new investigation.

The Rockefeller Establishment was frantic that its sacred cows might be butchered. The *Washington Post*, closely tied to the Rockefellers, never before known for its sense of public frugality, screamed that the Reece probe was "wholly unnecessary" and was "stupidly wasteful of public funds."

The heat was on. So much so that when in a speech on the floor of Congress Mr. Reece referred to a "conspiracy," his use of the term brought down on his head an avalanche of anger and ridicule from virtually the entire Establishment Press. At the same time, the foundations unleashed an enormous barrage of vilification against the probe.

While the Press was shouting "McCarthyism," Rockefeller elements in the Republican Party were working behind the scenes to kill the investigation. As Rene Wormser, counsel for the Reece Committee, noted in *Human Events* for July 5, 1969:

> A Republican President [Eisenhower, who had the full support of the Rockefellers in his fight against Robert Taft] sat in the White House. The House of Representatives and all its committees were Republican controlled. Mr. Reece was a distinguished and important Republican .... Yet, when a committee of five members was appointed to conduct the foundation investigation, Mr. Reece found that, of the four others appointed with him, three had been selected from among members of the House who had voted against the investigation.

The key agent in Rockefeller efforts to break up the investigation was Congressman Wayne Hays of Ohio, a member of the Committee. During the inquiry, two tennis-shoe types decided to play Agatha Christie and began trailing Hays. They discovered that he went to the same Washington hotel for a closed luncheon on a specific day each week. Dressing as cleaning women, the ladies investigated and established that Hays was reporting to representatives of several major foundations. Rene Wormser comments in *Human Events* on the Hays' tactics:

> Mr. Hays showed himself exceptionally adept at disruption. For example, in one session of 185 minutes, he resorted to constant interruption 246 times. He refused to obey rules of the committee. He insulted and vilified witnesses, counsel to the committee and committee members themselves. His intransigence finally caused a termination of the hearings.

The brazen Congressman Hays even explained the purpose of his conduct to Counsel Wormser. Mr. Wormser noted in his book, *Foundations: Their Power and Influence*: ". . . Mr. Hays told us one day that 'the White House' had been in touch with him and asked him if he would cooperate to kill the committee."

Because of limited time, staff, and money, the Reece Committee was forced to concentrate its investigation on various Rockefeller and Carnegie foundations, and on the huge Ford Foundation.

The Committee found that one of the first areas into which John D. invested his money was education. Daddy Oilbucks put his assistant, Fred Gates, in charge of his General Education Board. Gates tipped the Rockefeller philosophy on education in the Board's *Occasional Paper No. 1*:

> In our dreams we have limitless resources and the people yield themselves with perfect docility to our moulding hands. The present educational conventions fade from our minds, and unhampered by tradition, we work our own good will upon a grateful and responsive rural folk.

Later, the General Education Board expanded its horizons to take into its "moulding hands" the city folk as well. To this end the Rockefeller and Carnegie foundations, which often had interlocking directorates and many times acted in unison, began in the early Thirties to back John Dewey and his Marxist educationists with enormous amounts of money. As Rene Wormser observes:

> Research and experimental stations were established at selected universities, notably Columbia, Stanford, and Chicago. Here some of the worst mischief in recent education was born. In these Rockefeller-and-Carnegie-established vineyards worked many of the principal characters in the story of the suborning of American education. Here foundations nurtured some of the most ardent academic advocates of upsetting the American system and supplanting it with a Socialist state. . . .

The Carnegie and Rockefeller foundations had jumped into the financing of education and the social sciences with both Left feet. For example, the foundations (principally Carnegie and Rockefeller) stimulated two-thirds of the total endowment funding of all institutions of higher learning in America during the first third of this century. During this period the Carnegie-Rockefeller complex supplied twenty percent of the total income of colleges and universities and became in fact, if not in name, a sort of U. S. Ministry of Education. The result was a sharp Socialist-Fascist turn. As Rene Wormser, Counsel for the Reece Committee, reports:

> A very powerful complex of foundations and allied organizations has developed over the years to exercise a high degree of control over education. Part of this complex, and ultimately responsible for it, are the Rockefeller and Carnegie groups of foundations.

These foundations were, by way of grants amounting to hundreds of millions of dollars, responsible for the nation-wide acceptance of avowed socialist John Dewey's theories of progressive education and permissiveness — the products of which have been marching on our college campuses for the past two decades.

Traditionalist teachers, who had been strongly resisting Deweyism, were swamped by education propagandists backed with a flood of Rockefeller-Carnegie dollars. At the same time the National Education Association, the country's chief education lobby, was also financed largely by the Rockefeller and Carnegie foundations. It, too, threw its considerable weight behind the Dewey philosophies. As an NEA report maintained in 1934:

> A dying laissez-faire must be completely destroyed and all of us, including the "owners," must be subjected to a large degree of social control.

Since America's public school system was decentralized, the foundations had concentrated on influencing schools of education (particularly Columbia, the spawning ground for Deweyism), and on financing the writing of textbooks which were subsequently adopted nationwide. These foundation-produced textbooks were so heavily slanted in favor of socialism that Wormser concluded: "It is difficult to believe that the Rockefeller Foundation and the National Education Association could have supported these textbooks. But the fact is that Rockefeller financed them and the N.E.A. promoted them very widely."

Little wonder that Reece Committee Counsel Wormser says evidence compiled during and after the Reece investigation of foundations:

> . . . leads one to the conclusion that there was, indeed, something in the nature of an actual conspiracy among certain leading educators in the United States to bring about socialism through the use of our school systems. . .

Congressman Cox had denounced these foundations for precisely these reasons. He named in particular the Rockefeller Foundation, "whose funds have been used to finance individuals and organizations whose business it has been to get communism into the private and public schools of the country, to talk down America and play up Russia . . . ."

It goes without saying that, by controlling the textbooks, the progressivists gained an open sesame to the minds of millions of students in the government schools. As John T. Flynn observed, it wasn't necessary to poison every glass of water coming out of every tap in a given community. It was necessary only to drop one cup of poison into the reservoir.

So successful was this conspiracy that by June of 1955, the Progressive Education Association which had been founded by John Dewey officially disbanded. Dr. H. Gordon Hullfish, the Association's president, explained:

> Founded in 1919 the PEA was a protest movement against traditional education, based in large part upon the philosophy of John Dewey. One reason for PEA's end is that many of the practices it has advocated have been adopted by the nation's schools.

This progressive education is Rockefeller education. After all, they planned for it, they promoted it, and they paid for it!

Those who control education will over a period of several generations control a nation. The Rockefellers have for five or six decades been a controlling influence in the direction of American education.

While education is a powerful tool for controlling the thinking and outlook of people, it is not the only means. Religion is also an important moulder of public opinion.

For many years the Rockefeller Dynasty has bankrolled the Union Theological Seminary of New York, which has done so much to turn the clergy towards state socialism-fascism, and to destroy the tenets of traditional Christianity. The highly influential seminary is known for turning out "Christian-Communists."

The family's chief religious philanthropy for a number of years was the notorious Federal Council of Churches, which was pronounced by U.S. Naval Intelligence in 1936 as one of the most dangerous, subversive organizations in the country. According to Naval Intelligence:

> It is a large radical "pacifist" organization, and probably represents 20,000,000 Protestants in the United States. However, its leadership consists of a small group which dictates its policies. It is always extremely active in any matters against national defense.

In its many official pronouncements, the Federal Council attacked free enterprise, capitalism and the American way of life, and boldly advocated Socialism. In an official report in 1932, the Federal Council stated: "The Christian ideal calls for hearty support of a planned economic system. . . . It demands that cooperation shall replace competition as a fundamental method."

At a full meeting in Indianapolis in December, 1932, the Federal Council adopted unanimously this Socialist creed: "The churches should stand for social planning and control of the credit and monetary system and the economic processes."

The following year, 1933, the Council officially declared: "The Christian conscience can be satisfied with nothing less than the complete substitution of motives of mutual helpfulness and good will for the motive of private gain."

The Federal Council was so flagrantly a mouthpiece for the gospel according to St. Stalin that it was forced to change its name. It became the National Council of Churches which today claims to represent some forty million Protestants. While less prone to praising the Soviets as openly as its predecessor, the NCC has repeatedly been denounced by fundamentalist Christian organizations for its slavish adherence to promoting radical socialism and its lovey-dovey attitude toward Moscow. Today, after forty years of assiduous anti-Americanism and the promotion of totalitarian government at home and abroad, the NCC still enjoys the largesse of the Family Rockefeller. Its past president J. Irwin Miller is a perennial Rockefeller front man and a trustee of the Ford Foundation.*

Through its multiple foundations the Rockefeller family invested its money where it would have the most influence and do the family the most good. And by far the chief beneficiaries of its "charities" have been the Rockefellers.

---

*The NCC has donated hundreds of thousands of dollars to buy arms for revolutionary Communist groups in Africa. These arms are used by the Communists to slay Christians, while thousands of American clergymen look the other way. If this is not murder by proxy, what is it?

The question that is racing through the mind of most readers at this point undoubtedly is why the Rockefellers, considered the world's foremost capitalists, have spent hundreds of millions of dollars financing their alleged enemies, the socialists.

One would assume that, since the Rockefellers are thought of as *capitalists*, they would have used their fortune to foster the philosophy of individual liberty. But, just the opposite is true. We have been unable to find a single project in the history of the Rockefeller foundations which promotes free enterprise. Indeed, except in the fields of health and science (and some of these grants are highly questionable) almost all of the Rockefeller grants have been used directly or indirectly to promote economic and social collectivism, i.e., Socialism-Fascism.

Reasonable men ask what could motivate the Rockefellers to finance collectivist efforts which seem so totally at odds with their own interests. They forget that John D. Rockefeller was a Machiavellian who boasted that he hated competition. Whenever he could, Rockefeller used the government to promote his own interests and to hinder his competitors. Monopoly capitalism is impossible unless you have a government with the power to strangle would-be competitors.

The easiest way to control or eliminate competitors is not to best them in the marketplace, but to use the power of government to exclude them from the marketplace. If you wish to control commerce, banking, transportation, and natural resources on a national level, you must control the federal government. If you and your clique wish to establish worldwide monopolies, you must control a World Government.

The Rockefellers are not humanitarians; they are power-seeking Machiavellians. They are using their phony philanthropy as a guise for seizing power on a magnitude that would make old John D. Sr. proud.

Nelson Rockefeller, the unelected Vice President of the United States, is a leader in the campaign to submerge American sovereignty in a World Superstate. Long-time internationalist Alan Cranston (right) is also an avid promoter of World Government, in violation of his oath of office as a U.S. Senator.

At the center of *Insider* power, influence, and planning in the United States is the pervasive Council on Foreign Relations. Headquartered in the Harold Pratt House on 68th Street in New York City, its members have dominated the last seven Administrations and have com-

plete control of the Ford Administration now. The CFR was created by the Rockefellers and their allies to be the focus of their drive for a "New World Order."

Chapter Five
Yes, Virginia, There is an Establishment

The Rockefellers are the epitome of the nation's permanent Establishment: governments change, economics fluctuate, foreign alliances shift — the Rockefellers prevail.

Walter Cronkite
CBS Reports
"The Rockefellers"

In previous chapters we have seen that the Rockefellers exercise tremendous leverage over business, banking, and the economy. In the last chapter we showed how the family has used that money to set themselves up in the charity business, and then used their influence through their giveaways to guide education, religion, and the media—and therefore public opinion—along the proper course. Proper for the Rockefellers, that is.

The perfect situation, from the Rockefellers' point of view, is to combine their economic muscle and their political oomph so that one hand washes the other. They have mastered to a frightening degree the art of using economic power to build political power which enhances economic power even further, and so on, *ad infinitum*.

We have seen that the Rockefellers have spent generations developing an economic consortium that is the sleekest, smoothest, and most powerful combine on earth. The incredibly powerful political complex the Rockefellers have put together makes their economic activities look like the naive simplicity of a backwoods general store, and consists of organizations which are thoroughly interlocked with and financed by the House of Rockefeller.

While we hate to use the terribly trite cliché about the many arms of the octopus being controlled by the same brain, we apologetically must include it because it is simply the most apt analogy.

Some of these organizations, although they are *very* influential in government, are virtually unknown to the average citizen. Others you may hear cited by the media as a source for an important opinion or "inside information" about some national or international event. What you definitely are *not* told is that you are hearing the voice of Rockefeller under dozens of different guises from the family's loyal army of ventriloquists.

Collectively, this group of individuals and organizations is known as the Eastern Liberal Establishment; the key figures in it are often referred to as *Insiders*.

The keystone of the entire Establishment arch is the Council on Foreign Relations (CFR). The leadership of the CFR is the equivalent to the brain of the octopus. David Rockefeller is chairman of the board of the CFR. It is impossible to comprehend fully the interlock of Rockefeller power without being aware of the all-pervasive influence of the Council. So important is this organization that we will devote the rest of this chapter to it. And throughout the rest of this book we shall designate its members by putting CFR in parentheses after their names.

The Council on Foreign Relations, headquartered in New York City, is composed of an elite of approximately 1600 of the nation's Establishment *Insiders* in the fields of high finance, academics, politics, commerce, the foundations, and the mass media. The names of many of its members are household words; others, equally important, are less familiar. (For example, you may not recognize the name Harold Geneen. But when you hear he is chairman of the board of directors of IT&T, you can be assured he is a very big wheel indeed.)

Although the membership of the CFR is a veritable "Who's Who" in big business and the media, probably only one person in a thousand is familiar with the organization itself and even fewer are aware of its real purposes.

During its first fifty years of existence, the CFR was almost never mentioned by any of the moguls of the mass media. And when you realize that the membership of the CFR includes top executives from the *New York Times*, the *Washington Post*, the *Los Angeles Times*, the Knight newspaper chain, NBC, CBS, *Time*, *Life*, *Fortune*, *Business Week*, *U.S. News & World Report*, and many others, you can be sure that such anonymity is not accidental; it is deliberate.

For fifty years the CFR operated like the Invisible Man in the novel by H.G. Wells. In 1962, Dan Smoot's pioneering study, *The Invisible Government*, was successfully smothered by the paper curtain. Although its results were visible everywhere, the CFR seemed not to exist.

Then in 1972, two separate exposures of the Limousine Liberals of the CFR were published: *None Dare Call It Conspiracy* by this author, and *The Naked Capitalist* by Professor W. Cleon Skousen, former assistant to J. Edgar Hoover. Although both books were completely ignored by the Establishment's captive book review organs, both became nationwide bestsellers because of widespread interest in them at the grass roots level.

The fact that George Wallace was planning to seize upon the Council and its power, as an election-year issue in his third party candidacy for President, also contributed to the partial lifting of the cloak of secrecy which has surrounded the CFR. Obviously anticipating even more attention to the Council, two very similar articles on the CFR appeared in the *New York Times* and *New York* magazine. The strategy was to admit that the Council on Foreign Relations has long acted as the unelected supergovernment of the United States, but to maintain that it was always motivated by altruism, idealism, and selfless devotion to the public good. Moreover, the articles claimed, the CFR has, at least momentarily, withdrawn to the sidelines. Still, as John Franklin Campbell admitted in his magazine article:

> Practically every lawyer, banker, professor, general, journalist and bureaucrat who has had any influence on the foreign policy of the last six Presidents—from Franklin Roosevelt to Richard Nixon—has spent some time in the

Harold Pratt House, a four-story mansion on the corner of Park Avenue and 68th Street, donated 26 years ago by Mr. Pratt's widow [*an heir to the Standard Oil fortune*] to the Council on Foreign Relations, Inc. . . .

If you can walk—or be carried—into the Pratt House, it usually means that you are a partner in an investment bank or law firm—with occasional "trouble-shooting" assignments in government. You believe in foreign aid, NATO, and a bipartisan foreign policy. *You've been pretty much running things in this country for the last 25 years, and you know it.* [*Emphasis added*]

Establishment apologist Anthony Lukas, writing in the *New York Times* magazine, also admitted that the *Insiders* of the Council have been responsible for our disastrous foreign policy over the past twenty-five years:

From 1945 well into the sixties, Council members were in the forefront of America's globalist activism: the United Nations organizational meeting in San Francisco (John McCloy, Hamilton Fish Armstrong, Joseph Johnson, Thomas Finletter and many others),* as ambassadors to the world body (Edward Stettinius, Henry Cabot Lodge, James Wadsworth and all but three others); the U.S. occupation in Germany (Lucius Clay as military governor, McCloy again and James Conant as High Commissioners); NATO (Finletter again, Harlan Cleveland, Charles Spofford as U.S. delegates).

For the last three decades, American foreign policy has remained largely in the hands of men—the overwhelming majority of them Council members—whose world perspective was formed in World War II and in the economic reconstructions and military security programs that followed. . . . The Council was their way of staying in touch with the levels of power . . . .

Prior to this time the number of stories about the CFR appearing in the mass media could be counted on the fingers of one hand. One of these early articles appeared in

---

*One of the "many other" CFR members active in the founding of the UN, whom Mr. Lukas did *not* mention, was the notorious traitor, perjurer, and Soviet agent, Alger Hiss, who actually served as Secretary General of the San Francisco meeting.

Harper's magazine in July 1958, and it is revealing to look at it now because its author, "Liberal" columnist Joseph Kraft, was himself a member of the CFR, and he was obviously directing his message to potential members of the Establishment's exclusive circle. Describing the influence of the CFR, Kraft said:

> It has been the seat of . . . basic government decisions, has set the context for many more, and has repeatedly served as a recruiting ground for ranking officials.

It is worth noting that Kraft called his article "School for Statesmen"—an admission that the members of the Council learn a "line" of strategy to be pursued in Washington.

Indeed, the CFR has served as a virtual employment agency for the federal government, under both Democrat and Republican administrations. In his *New York Times* magazine article, Anthony Lukas observed: ". . . everyone knows how fraternity brothers can help other brothers climb the ladder of life. If you want to make foreign policy, there's no better fraternity to belong to than the Council. . . ." This "fraternity" of *Insiders* has been so successful that its members have virtually dominated *every administration* in Washington since the days of Franklin Delano Roosevelt. CFR members occupied the major policy-making positions, especially in the field of foreign relations, under Roosevelt, Truman, Eisenhower, Kennedy, Johnson, and Nixon; and they are just as powerful today, under the Administration of Gerald Ford.

As Joseph Kraft phrased it: "the Council plays a special part in helping to bridge the gap between the two parties, affording unofficially a measure of continuity when the guard changes in Washington."

George Wallace made famous the slogan that there is not a dime's worth of difference between the Democrat and Republican parties. Many observers have noted that while the two parties use different rhetoric and aim their spiels at differing segments of the population, it seems to make little difference who actually wins the election. The reason for this is that while grass roots Democrats and Republicans generally have greatly differing views on the economy, political policies, and federal activities, as you climb the sides of the political pyramid the two parties become more and more alike. The reason there isn't a dime's worth of difference is that instead of having two distinctly different groups called Democrats and Republicans, we actually have Rockedems and Rockepubs.

Every four years the Americans have the privilege of choosing between the Rockepubs candidate and the Rockedems standard bearer. In 1952 and 1956, CFR Adlai Stevenson challenged CFR Eisenhower. In 1960, it was CFR Nixon vs. CFR Kennedy. In 1964, the conservative wing of the GOP stunned the Establishment by nominating its candidate over Nelson Rockefeller. At which point Rockefeller and the CFR wing proceeded to picture Barry Goldwater as a dangerous radical who would abolish Social Security, drop atom bombs on Hanoi, and in general be a reincarnation of the Fascist dictator Mussolini. The CFR Rockepubs drew up the indictment, the Rockedems prosecuted the case, and Goldwater went down to ignominious defeat—without ever understanding how he had been sandbagged by the leaders of his own party.

Having disposed of the challenge to the Establishment in 1964, the CFR was firmly back in the saddle in 1968. That year CFR Nixon was "pitted" against CFR Humphrey. The 1972 "contest" featured CFR Nixon vs. CFR McGovern. The Rockefellers were sure to win no matter which candidate emerged victorious.

In recent years, Establishment apologists would have you believe that the CFR was thrust into the cold by Richard Nixon (one such article was even titled "The Death Rattle of the Eastern Establishment"). Such protestations are about as sincere as Br'er Rabbit begging not to be thrown into the briar patch.

The truth is that Nixon was completely under the thumb of the CFR, and served his masters faithfully—until they abandoned him to open the White House doors for Nelson Rockefeller as an *unelected* Vice President. At the beginning of his Administration, Nixon placed at least 115 CFR members in key positions in the Executive Branch—an all-time high for any President. The vast majority of these men are still around today, running the Ford Administration.

Perhaps the most important and certainly the most prominent of all these Establishment *Insiders* is Henry Kissinger. No man alive could more effectively represent the Council on Foreign Relations than Herr Kissinger, who for all practical purposes has emerged as the Assistant President of the United States. Kissinger was a Rockefeller man, serving on the staff of the CFR, when he received his appointment to the Nixon Administration.

Kissinger has long recognized how much he owes to the Council on Foreign Relations. In the preface to his book *The Necessity For Choice*, published in 1961, he said:

> Five years ago, the Council on Foreign Relations gave me my first opportunity to work systematically on problems of foreign relations. My relations with it have remained close and my admiration for it has, if anything, increased.

Consider: In 1956, Kissinger was an obscure German immigrant who was a mere professor at Harvard University. In less than twenty years, he has become so powerful that he survives the dismissal of his ostensible boss, and apparently tells presidents, prime ministers, and other potentates what to say and do. What is the source of his remarkable authority?

Professor Kissinger's public commitments were in nearly every case the opposite of those expressed by Richard Nixon in his successful bid for the Presidency. But, after the rah-rah of the campaign was over, the CFR boys were brought in to run the show—and Henry Kissinger was Numero Uno.

Richard Nixon's own membership in the Council on Foreign Relations became an issue in 1962, during his contest with Joe Shell in California for the Republican gubernatorial nomination. After that, Mr. Nixon arranged with the Council for his name not to appear on public releases as a member. The CFR admits that it is sometimes necessary for its members to appear to have left the Council. On page 42 of the Council's 1952 Report, for example, we read:

> Members of the Council are sometimes obliged, by their acceptance of government posts in Washington and elsewhere, to curtail or suspend for a time their participation in Council activities.

Was Richard Nixon a secret member of the CFR throughout his Presidency? The Reece Congressional Committee discovered during its investigation of foundations that there are a number of secret members of the Council, including industrialist Cyrus Eaton and Senator William Fulbright. Our guess is that Richard Nixon was among them.

Consider, after all, Mr. Nixon's CFR foreign policy — a subject in which he has certainly earned his scarlet "A." Disarmament without inspections, increased "trade" on credit with the Communists, abandonment of our anti-Communist allies, *detente* with the Soviet Union and Red China, are all programs of the CFR. Every one of these policies contradicts the Republican Party Platform of 1968. But, once in the White House, Mr. Nixon ignored the Republican Platform on which he was elected and proceeded to follow the dictates of the Council on Foreign Relations.

What are the Rockefellers attempting to accomplish with their CFR?

For the first time we now have an actual member of the CFR who is willing to testify against the organization. He is Admiral Chester Ward, U.S. Navy (Ret.), who as a hotshot youngish Admiral had become Judge Advocate General of the Navy. As a "man on the rise" he was invited to become a member of the "prestigious" CFR. The Establishment obviously assumed that Admiral Ward, like so many hundreds before him, would succumb to the flattery of being invited into the inner sanctums of the

Establishment, and that through subtle appeals to personal ambition would quickly fall in line. The *Insiders* badly underestimated the toughness and stern character of Admiral Ward. He soon became a vocal opponent of the organization. And while the Rockefellers were not so gauche as to remove him from the rolls of the organization, he is no longer invited to attend the private luncheons and briefing sessions. The Admiral states:

> The objective of the influential majority of members of CFR has not changed since its founding in 1922, more than 50 years ago. In the 50th anniversary issue of *Foreign Affairs* [the official quarterly publication of the CFR], the first and leading article was written by CFR member Kingman Brewster, Jr., entitled "Reflections on Our National Purpose." He did not back away from defining it: *our national purpose should be to abolish our nationality.* Indeed, he pulled out all the emotional stops in a hardsell for global government. He described our "Vietnam-seared generation" as being "far from America Firsters"—an expression meant as a patronizing sop to our young people. In the entire CFR lexicon, there is no term of revulsion carrying a meaning so deep as "America First."

While CFR members are not robots and may disagree on many minor matters, according to the Admiral, this "lust to surrender" our independence is common to most of them:

> Although, from the inside, CFR is certainly not the monolith that some members and most nonmembers consider it, this lust to surrender the sovereignty and independence of the United States is pervasive throughout most of the membership, and particularly in the leadership of the several divergent cliques . . . .

If the Rockefeller family's CFR has a "passion to surrender" U.S. sovereignty, to whom are we supposed to surrender? Admiral Ward answers that the goal is the "submergence of U.S. sovereignty and national independence into an all-powerful one-world government." And, according to the Admiral, about 95 percent of the 1,600 members of the CFR are aware that this is the real purpose of the Council—and support that goal!

For centuries, naive idealists have dreamed of a "parliament of man" that would put an end to poverty, ignorance and disease. Modern one-worlders have added pollution and over-population to the list of evils World Government would cure. The allure of a world super-state to such starry-eyed dreamers is obvious.

But what is the appeal of a World Government to such canny rationalists as the Rockefellers and others of the international super-rich? You might think that such a World Government would threaten their financial power and therefore would be the last thing on earth they would support. The answer is obvious—they expect the coming World Government to be under their control!

You will remember that John D. Rockefeller, Sr., who proclaimed that "competition is a sin," used every devious trick he could devise to create a *national* oil monopoly. His strategy was as ruthless as it was effective: *Get* control of your competitors, and then *keep* control of them.

Old John D. quickly learned that political power was essential to protect and advance his economic clout, so he went into the politics business. Once he controlled the purse strings of enough captive Congressmen, he could get them to pull strings to benefit Standard Oil and the family's other business interests. In other words, he sought *national* control to protect his *national* monopoly.

Today, however, the Rockefeller interests are not just nationwide, they are worldwide. Both Exxon and Chase Manhattan Bank do business in more than one hundred countries. The majority of these countries are found in what is euphemistically called the "third world." Many of these are former colonies of Western nations who owe their so-called independence to the Rockefellers and the CFR. Now they are ruled, for the most part, by tin-pot dictators who have no more understanding of the realities of economics than Elizabeth Taylor does of the sanctity of a convent. And there is always the chance that one of these new "people's republics" will forget who owns them.

An even greater danger to the internationalists of the CFR, however, is the fear that enough Americans will finally understand what they are doing and, in the age-old tradition of an angry electorate, "throw the rascals out." Faced with the possibility that any one of a hundred mini-nations might suddenly thumb its nose at you; or even worse, that the citizens of your own country might get wise to the game plan and give you the heave-ho, what do you do?

The answer has been obvious to the Rockefellers for more than fifty years: you create a one-world government which you will control, and you have that government rule all the others.

This has been the game plan for at least the past 54 years—ever since Daddy Oilbucks himself donated money to build the League of Nations headquarters in Geneva. Unfortunately for his own ambitions, there were still enough un-bought Senators and un-controlled news-papers in the United States to thwart his plans. His countrymen escaped the noose he and his comrades had prepared for them by refusing to join the budding World Government.

But the conspirators learned their lesson and did not make the same mistake again. They went to work at once, first, by creating the Council on Foreign Relations, and then by using it to soften up the U.S. for the next World Government they would propose.*

The *Insiders* cloak their grasp for world political power in many idealistic cliches, and hide their true intentions behind a number of code phrases. The current favorite seems to be "New World Order."

The expression is as old as the diabolical scheme of a secret society of the Eighteenth Century called the Illuminati, for a *novus ordo seclorum*—in fact, "new world order" is merely a translation of the Illuminati's avowed goal.

By 1945, the Rockefellers were ready. Grandson Nelson was one of the 74 CFR members at the founding meeting of the United Nations in San Francisco. Later, Nelson and

---

*For more details about this whole plot, read *None Dare Call It Conspiracy* by this author.

his brothers donated the land for the United Nations complex along the East River in New York—possibly because they did not want the new headquarters of their World Government to be more than a short taxi-ride away from their penthouses.

Such a "New World Order" most emphatically does not mean an impotent debating society to the CFR. It means an international regime that controls the world's armies, the world's weapons, its courts, its tax collectors, its schools, its governments and everything else. In succeeding chapters we will see exactly how the Rockefellers intend to nurture their embryonic structure until it has all of these powers, and more. For the moment, take our word that the "New World Order" these international wheeler-dealers have in mind would *not* be a republic, bound down by the chains of a constitution (as Jefferson phrased it), working to increase freedom for all of us, where the rights of every citizen are protected from a tyrannical Big Brother.

The "New World Order" the Rockefellers are planning will be a world dictatorship. Conservatives will call it Socialism or Communism, Liberals will call it Fascism. The label makes little difference; it will be the Gulag Archipelago on a worldwide basis.

Of course, proponents of such a World Government disguise their intentions behind all kinds of double talk. For example, Senator Alan Cranston of California (for many years the president of the Rockefeller-interlocked United World Federalists), defended his proposal for a world super-state with these words:

> (World Government) Proposition 64 does not propose that we give up a shred of sovereignty. Plainly it proposes a means by which we can gain the ability to exercise our presently impotent sovereignty in the vital area of war prevention. It proposes that we create a limited world government and deposit our sovereignty there . . . .

Let us repeat that. Senator Cranston says we won't "give up a shred of sovereignty" if we "create a limited world government and deposit our sovereignty there."

Lewis Carroll couldn't have said it better. George Orwell didn't even try; he called it "newspeak."

But while Senator Cranston and many of his colleagues play the string section in the orchestration for World Government, other CFR members trumpet other parts in this carefully rehearsed symphony. Nelson Rockefeller, for example, as an "altruistic millionaire," sounds the melody line for international taxation. In his book *The Future of Federalism*, first published in 1962 and then reprinted when he was nominated for the Vice Presidency, Nelson stated: ". . . I think the answer is some free-world super-national political being with the power to tax. . . ." Ask yourself this question: Does Nelson Rockefeller want to tax *his* wealth to aid the world's poor? If so, why doesn't he eliminate those expensive bureaucratic middlemen, and simply give his money to the downtrodden masses now? Is it possible that he is trying to become richer—wads and wads richer, as the family representative put it — by dividing *your* wealth with himself?

During the confirmation hearings over his nomination as the nation's second unelected Vice President, a few courageous Congressmen, such as Representative John Ashbrook and Senator Jesse Helms, asked how it would be possible for Nelson to uphold an oath to protect and defend the Constitution of the United States when he was already on record as supporting a World Government that would scrap our national charter. Such inquiries, however, were ignored by both Rockefeller and the national media. You would think that the issue of the survival of the United States might rate a line or two in your local Daily Bugle. But instead, all of the space was given to a planned farce about whether or not Rocky financed a derogatory book about a political opponent. That's like launching a newspaper crusade accusing Jack the Ripper of throwing gum wrappers in the gutter and ignoring his penchant for slitting throats!

In *The Future of Federalism*, Noble Nels proclaimed:

No nation today can defend its freedom, or fulfill the needs and aspirations of its own people, from within its own borders or through its own resources alone . . . . And so the nation-state, standing alone, threatens, in many ways, to seem as anachronistic as the Greek city-states eventually became in ancient times.

Get it? The man who could not be elected to the White House, but managed to arrange an entrance there anyway, says that a free and independent United States is now "anachronistic." Webster's defines "anachronism" as "something from a former age that is incongruous in the present."

Every effective World Government proponent learns early in the game some rhetorical tricks, such as calling black white. Nelson Rockefeller is no exception. In the same book, he suggests:

> The federal idea, which our Founding Fathers applied in their historic act of political creation in the eighteenth century, can be applied in this twentieth century in the larger context of the world of free nations—if we will but match our forefathers in courage and vision.

Even Nelson Rockefeller knows that the American Revolution was a protest against exactly the sort of centralized power he himself now advocates. The British Empire was the World Government of its day. Our forefathers did not want to be *inter*-dependent; they wanted to be independent. And they were willing to pay the price for their independence in the same coin that free men must always be willing to pay—blood and gold.

During the early 1950's, Nelson Rockefeller encouraged the wide distribution of a photograph of himself. It showed him holding a globe in his hands, and staring pensively into the future. Many people are convinced that the symbolism involved was *not* accidental.

Chapter Six
The Rockefeller Mediacracy

*Equally important is CFR's influence in the mass
media . . . . They control or own major newspapers,
magazines, radio and television networks . . .*

Admiral Chester Ward
(CFR and USN, Retired)

The Rockefellers, as we have seen, have never been
ones to leave public opinion to chance. That is why they
have invested their charitable monies so judiciously in
education and religion. It would be naive to think that the
family would not exert every possible subtle and unsubtle
influence over the nation's mass media.

In Chapter One we described how the Rockefellers use
leverage to maximize the power of their investments in industry and finance. They follow the same principle when
they buy influence over education. They do not pour
money into local school board races; they put their bucks
into the schools that train the teachers and they finance
the writing of textbooks. Now that every public school is
at the mercy of the Department of Health, Education and
Welfare (which Nelson Rockefeller created and ran under
Eisenhower), the family couldn't care less who controls
the local school board. In the field of religion, the money
goes to key seminaries where ministers are trained and
to the National Council of Churches which claims to represent forty million Protestants.

The Rockefellers grab, with all the gusto they've got, at
the *apex* of whatever instrumentality they wish to control.
The influence of the Council on Foreign Relations in the
federal government is concentrated in the Executive
Branch. That is where the action is—at the top. And so it is
with Rockefeller control of the media. They are not
interested in controlling the Burnt Mattress Weekly Blat;

they go for the leaders in the field. In the old days, John D. sent his agents out to bribe editors and to buy up small papers, but that is very inefficient and antiquated in the electronic age. Now, the local papers are dependent on wire services and syndicated columnists to fill their news and editorial pages.

The Rockefellers have made sure that the real movers and shakers in the field of mass communications have been initiated into their CFR lodge. Admiral Ward informs us:

> Equally important is CFR's influence in the mass media. Out of its 1,551 members, 60 were listed in official CFR reports as engaged in "journalism." An additional 61 were listed in "communications management," a highly descriptive title, because CFR members do indeed "manage" mass communications media, especially the *influential segments*. They control or own major newspapers, magazines, radio and television networks, and they control the most powerful companies in the book publishing business.

Few would argue the fact that the *New York Times* is the most influential newspaper in the U.S. "A significance of the *Times*," Timesman James Reston has written, "is its multiplier effect. What appears in the *Times* automatically appears later in other places."

Concerning this multiplier effect, Alice Widener, columnist for *Barron's*, notes:

> It is a fact that most editors and newsmen on the staffs of *Life*, *Look*, *Time*, *Newsweek*, etc., and most editors, reporters, and commentators at NBC, CBS, and ABC take their news and editorial cues from the *New York Times*. Technically, it is a great newspaper; but it reports much of the news in conformity with its editorial policies.

The late Arthur Hays Sulzberger, chairman of the board of the *New York Times*, was a member of the CFR, and today there are at least 11 people in high positions with the *Times* who are CFR members. Sulzberger's son-in-law Orvil E. Dryfoos (CFR) succeeded him as publisher. The current publisher is Arthur Ochs "Punch" Sulzberger (CFR).

Other CFR members at the *Times* are: Harding Bancroft, Executive Vice President; James Reston, Vice President and columnist; A. M. Rosenthal, managing editor; Seymour Topping, assistant managing editor; Max Frankel, Sunday editor; Harrison Salisbury, associate editor; C. L. Sulzberger, columnist; and David Halberstam, columnist.

The *Times* is infamous for its anti-anti-Communism and its support of socialist-fascist legislation. Its treatment of Stalin as a kindly liberal running a Russian branch of the ACLU should have made it a laughing stock, but didn't. Neither did the *Times'* Herbert L. Matthews' (CFR) treatment of "Dr. Castro" as the George Washington of Cuba. Matthews swore repeatedly that Castro was anything but a Communist. Later, jokers commented that Castro could honestly say, "I got my job through the *New York Times*."

Needless to say, the support Nelson Rockefeller has received in his political career from the normally Democrat *Times* has been nearly total.

Running a close second to the *New York Times* in the prestige race is the *Washington Post*. Every Senator and Congressman, regardless of his party or political persuasion, has the *Post* on his desk each morning. Like the *Times*, the *Post* is read by the people who count when it comes to running the country. The *Post's* owner and publisher Katharine Graham is a member of the CFR, as are other top editors and management personnel. For years the *Post* has been referred to as "the uptown Daily Worker." The only time the *Post* has ever opposed "big government" is when it has been used to investigate Communism. When this has happened, the people at the *Post* frantically start waving the Constitution and babbling about "freedom of speech"—something they regularly suppress when it involves opposition to fascism-socialism or the Rockefellers.

One of the most influential members of the *Post's* staff is the incredibly talented truth-twister, cartoonist Herbert L. Block. Herblock's cartoons are syndicated daily in hundreds of papers. (And for every person who reads the editorial page, there are probably a hundred who look at the lead cartoon.)

The *Los Angeles Times* is the West Coast's most important newspaper. Formerly staunchly conservative, the paper made a sharp Left turn fifteen years ago and while it still retains its GOP standing for protective coloring, it has become an organ for Establishment socialism. The *Times* is connected to the Rockefellers' CFR through board chairman Franklin Murphy and the fact that it owns a wire service in conjunction with the ultra-Liberal *Washington Post*. In addition, the *Los Angeles Times* owns the important *Newsday* on Long Island.

Other major newspapers with CFR interlocks are: the *Arkansas Gazette*, *Des Moines Register & Tribune*, Gannett Co. (publisher of newspapers in 40 cities from New York to Hawaii), *The Houston Post*, *Minneapolis Star & Tribune*, *The Denver Post* and *Louisville Courier*.*

Equally important has been CFR influence within the wire services. For many years Arthur Sulzberger was a director of the Associated Press while today Katharine Graham and John Cowles, Jr. are on the board. In addition, the *New York Times* has its own news service as does the *Washington Post-Los Angeles Times*. Every daily newspaper in the country uses one or more of these wire services for news and editorials.

Today it might be argued that television has superceded the newspaper as the primary creator of public opinion. Naturally, the Rockefellers have reached for control of the tube. William S. Paley, chairman of the board of CBS, is a CFR member as well as a trustee of the Ford Foundation. CBS has over 200 TV and 255 radio affiliates nationwide. CBS's president, Arthur Taylor, and Michael O'Neill of CBS publications are both members of the CFR. The former president of CBS was Dr. Frank Stanton

---

*There are more than thirty Committees on Foreign Relations in major U.S. cities which the CFR says are "affiliated" with the Council. Members of these local CFR Committees staff scores of other newspapers and radio-television stations.

(CFR), who is also a trustee of the Rockefeller Foundation and Carnegie Institution. CBS directors who are CFR members include Roswell Gilpatrick, Courtney Brown, Henry Schacht, and William Burden. CBS (sometimes referred to as the Conspiracy Brainwashing System) newsmen who are CFR members include Charles C. Collingwood, Richard C. Hottelet, Marvin Kalb, Larry LeSueur, and Daniel Schorr.*

The National Broadcasting Company is a subsidiary of the Radio Corporation of America. Until his recent retirement, the head of RCA-NBC was long-time CFR member David Sarnoff. Like CBS's Paley, Sarnoff was born in Russia. Under him, RCA was a major financial contributor to the CFR. Sarnoff spent much of his time promoting "foreign aid." Succeeding David Sarnoff at RCA is son Robert, a director of the Advertising Council, a spinoff of the CFR.

NBC newsmen John Chancellor and Irving R. Levine are CFR members, as are directors Thornton Bradshaw and John Petty.

The American Broadcasting Company is the Tag-Along Tooloo of the Big Three networks. It has 153 TV stations and specializes in escapist entertainment. It generally leaves the "documentary" propaganda to the Big Two. Its news audience amounts to only 7 million, while the other networks divide up the remaining 35 million news watchers. It does not have the CFR ties that CBS and NBC do, but Chase Manhattan Bank controls 6.7 percent of its stock—enough to give it a controlling interest. Chase,

---

*Certainly no one was very surprised that CBS carried an almost unprecedented 2-hour propaganda show on "The Rockefellers" during prime viewing time on Friday, December 28, 1973. CBS used its star, Walter Cronkite, to narrate this spectacle, which was so sugary it must have sent thousands of diabetics scrambling for their insulin. Cronkite closed by saying that if any family had to have as much money and power as the Rockefellers, it was a good thing it was the Rockefellers! For a political candidate to buy that kind of television time would cost an astronomical sum. But Rocky has friends. It didn't cost him a nickel.

through its trust department, controls 14 percent of CBS and 4.5 percent of RCA. Instead of three competing television networks called NBC, CBS, and ABC, what we really have is the Rockefeller Broadcasting Company, the Rockefeller Broadcasting System, and the Rockefeller Broadcasting Consortium.

Although the advent of television has somewhat diminished the influence of the slick magazines upon mass opinion, their importance is still significant. Until its demise (caused by advertisers switching to television), the nation's second-leading magazine in circulation was *Look*, with 7,750,000 copies distributed per issue. *Look* was owned by Cowles Communications, headed by Gardner and John Cowles. Both Cowles brothers are members of the Council on Foreign Relations.

The Cowles publishing empire encompasses *Harper's*, a list of trade journals, a string of newspapers and television stations, and Harper & Row. Managing the operation for the Cowles family is Cass Canfield of the CFR and World Federalists. John Cowles is married to Canfield's daughter.

John Cowles runs the *Minneapolis Tribune* and *Des Moines Register*. He is a trustee of the Rockefeller-interlocked Carnegie Endowment for International Peace and of the Ford Foundation, and he is a member of the National Policy Board of American Assembly — a front created by Averell Harriman, the Ford and Rockefeller Foundations, and the CFR to run propaganda seminars for leaders in American business, labor, communications, and the academy. He is on the Advisory Council of the U.S. Committee for the U.N. and the ultra-Leftist National Committee for an Effective Congress, which operates a "be kind to the Communists" lobby in Washington.

According to the American Legion's *Firing Line* of August 15, 1954, John Cowles joined twenty-three others signing telegrams to U.S. Senators "asking support of measures which would stifle all Congressional investigations of Communism." Little wonder, Brother John is very serious about merging America into a World Government with the Communists. The following is from a U.P.I. dispatch of June 7, 1959:

> John Cowles, publisher of "The Minneapolis Star and Tribune" said today that the traditional American concept of national sovereignty is obsolete. . . .

Gardner Cowles, chairman of the board of Cowles Communications, works hard to keep up with the Leftist activities of his brother. Besides being a member of the CFR, he is also a member of the Atlantic Union Committee.

Running *Look* magazine for the Cowles boys was William Atwood (CFR), who once wrote that we could "thank our lucky stars that Castro is not a Communist."

What Americans can thank their lucky stars about is that *Look*, which published more smears against anti-Communists than any other publication outside the official Communist Press, went broke.

After nearly four decades as a leading opinion maker in America, *Life* bit the same dust as *Look* and for the same reason, despite a whopping circulation of 8.5 million. *Life's* corporate brother, *Time*, the leading newsweekly, with a circulation of 4.2 million (as compared to *Newsweek's* 2.5 million and *U.S. News & World Report's* 1.8) is healthy, as are Time Inc.'s *Sports Illustrated* and *Fortune*.

The Time corporation recently bought its first newspaper, the *Newark Evening News*, for $34 million, and later purchased thirty-two more in the Chicago suburbs. It also owns Little, Brown & Company, an Establishment book publisher; 300,000 shares of Metro-Goldwyn-Mayer; 600,000 acres of timberland; and, is part owner of media in South America, West Germany, Hong Kong, and Australia. In addition to all this, Time Inc. owns some thirty television stations in America, giving this mammoth conglomerate a voice in every form of mass media—newspapers, magazines, movies, television, book publishing, and even teaching machines.

The builder of this empire was the late Henry Luce (CFR), whose impact on American thinking has been enormous. As Theodore White (CFR) has noted, "He . . . revolutionized the thinking of American readers." Luce started his rise to publishing glory with loans from CFR-Establishmentarians Thomas Lamont and Dwight Morrow (like Lamont, a J. P. Morgan partner), Harvey Firestone, E. Roland Harriman, and various members of the Harkness family (Standard Oil fortune). Their influence became especially apparent when he started his business magazine, *Fortune*, in the middle of the depression. As John Kobler writes in *The First Tycoon*:

> . . . It is a bemusing paradox that *Fortune*, the magazine of business, questioned the efficiency of the free-enterprise system and even took on a faint socialist tinge. Some of its editors and contributors stood far to the left. . . .

Apparently that is what Luce's Rockefeller-connected financial angels wanted. And, although he later seemed to oppose F.D.R., Henry Luce cheered his accomplishments: "I didn't vote for F.D.R. but it was all right with me that he won. He accomplished a lot of necessary social reform."

Jeanne Harmon, a former *Life* staff writer, tells in *Such Is Life* how tolerant Luce was of the Communist cell openly working at Time-Life. Mrs. Harmon relates how headlines were suddenly altered to convey meanings never intended, and how she and her fellow reporters were subjected to pressures to ignore some stories and push others. She also reveals that Whittaker Chambers was not welcomed back to Time-Life after he had testified against Alger Hiss (CFR).

Henry Luce was at one time actually considered an anti-Communist. Yet he always bitterly opposed anyone like Robert Taft, General Douglas MacArthur, or Barry Goldwater, whom he thought might actually *do* something about Communist subversion in the United States. Luce's bogus anti-Communism was used to promote his World Government crusades. He was a member of the CFR and the Atlantic Union. Henry Luce was also a strong supporter of the United Nations, even after Alger Hiss's role in its establishment was revealed.

In the late Fifties, Henry Luce switched from the "World Government to oppose Communism" line to the "peaceful co-existence and World Government with Communism" line, and *Life* went back to glorifying the Soviet Union as it had done during World War II. In 1966, Luce took a group of 43 U.S. businessmen behind the Iron Curtain to promote aid and trade with the enemy.

The chairman at Time Inc. is Andrew Heiskell (CFR), who is married to a *New York Times* heiress.

Editor-in-chief of all Time Inc. publications is Hedley Donovan, a Rhodes Scholar, former reporter for the Limousine Leftist *Washington Post*, and a member of the CFR. Other CFR-Establishmentarians in the Time Inc. hierarchy are vice chairman Roy Larsen and directors John Gardner and Sol Linowitz.

The CFR members of Time Inc. also include James Linen, chairman of *Time's* executive committee; vice presidents Otto Fuerbringer and Barry Zorthian and directors Frank Pace, Jr. and Rawleigh Warner. So closely is Time Inc. now linked with the Rockefellers that the two jointly own a helicopter.

Rapidly closing the circulation gap with *Time* is *Newsweek*. *Newsweek* is owned by the *Washington Post*. Chairman of the board Frederick Beebe is a member of the CFR as was the late owner, Katharine Graham's son Phillip. Retired editor Malcolm Muir is a CFR member, as are current editors Osborn Elliot and Robert Christopher, and vice president Nicholas Katzenbach. Other CFR men at *Newsweek* are editorial page editor Philip Geyelin, columnist Stewart Alsop, contributing editor Carl Spaatz, Atlanta Bureau chief William Anderson, and directors Katharine Graham and Kermit Lansner.

Other magazines in the CFR orbit are *Business Week*, *Atlantic Monthly*, *McCalls*, *World Review* (formerly *Saturday Review of Literature*) and *Scientific American*.*

---

*One of the most curious publications to join the list of CFR interlocked journals is the ostensibly conservative magazine *National Review*. Although *National Review* has in the past

Book publishers with representatives on the CFR include MacMillan, Random House, Simon & Schuster, McGraw-Hill, Harper Brothers, IBM Publishing and Printing, Xerox Corp., Yale University Press and Harper & Row. Many of these specialize in publishing textbooks. The Book of the Month Club's chairman Axel Rosin is a member of the CFR.

Given this kind of power over the media, it is hardly surprising that the Rockefeller family generally gets the powder puff treatment from the media. The interlocking CFR web woven by the Rockefellers explains why Nelson received such unanimous hosannas from the media during his hearings for the Vice Presidency. Though a few individual reporters were mildly critical of some facets of Nelson's career, the managers of the major papers and magazines positively drooled over themselves at the prospect of Sir Nelson the Fair being a heartbeat away from the Presidency. This is not exactly the tone used on Barry Goldwater in 1964. The one-eyed press is a Rockefeller-controlled Cyclops.

There is yet another power the Dynasty has over the mass media. The average newspaper depends on advertising for from two-thirds to three-fourths of its revenues. Ike McAnally, for four decades a reporter with the *New York Daily News*, comments in *Counterattack*:

---

claimed to be an opponent of the Eastern Liberal Establishment, it has never called attention to the conspiratorial activities of the Rockefeller Dynasty — and, in fact, has bitterly ridiculed anyone who suggested that there were any conspiratorial wolves mixed in with the Liberal sheep. Many well-informed conservatives were puzzled by *National Review's* refusal to consider the possibility that most of the liberal "mistakes" the magazine decried were actually carefully planned and deliberate acts; their bewilderment is bound to increase when they learn that editor-in-chief William F. Buckley, Jr., who has boasted of his personal friendship and warm admiration for such important *Insiders* as Henry Kissinger, and who enthusiastically endorsed Nelson Rockefeller for Secretary of Defense, is himself a member of the Council on Foreign Relations.

The most persistent influence upon the editorial policies of metropolitan newspapers today is the large advertiser. In many instances these advertisers are department stores. Some of these make open and contemptuous demands upon the front offices of newspapers to support the left wing. Others relay "suggestions." . .-.

. . . Newspapers have surrendered unconditionally to left wing front office pressures, real and imaginary. . . .

. . . They realize that if they write a story which might draw unfavorable reaction from, for instance, a department store, the city editor is apt to throw their copy back at them. . . . It is inevitable that with front offices swinging over, individual newsmen have more elastic principles.

Here's how it works. Every one of the major department store chains—R. H. Macy & Company, Federated Department Stores, Gimbel Brothers, Sears, Roebuck & Company, J. C. Penney Company, The May Department Stores Company, Interstate Department Stores, and Allied Stores Corporation—has on its board of directors at least one officer who is a member of the Council on Foreign Relations and/or a partner in the CFR interlocked international banking firms such as Kuhn, Loeb; Lazard Freres; Lehman Brothers; Dillon, Read & Company; or Goldman Sachs.

Department stores, of course, are not the only buyers of advertising space. Oil companies are also biggies. So are banks. As are the myriad of corporations listed in the early part of this book as under Rockefeller family domination.

Establishment adventurers will, of course, permit a paper to take a moderately conservative stand, but it is taboo to discuss the Rockefeller Establishment and its links with the International Communist Conspiracy.

With all of this membership in America's key mass media, it can hardly be an accident that few people know about the Council on Foreign Relations. If the Rockefellers wanted publicity for the CFR you can bet there would be feature spreads in *Time* and *Newsweek* plus a "60 Minute" CBS Special narrated by Walter Cronkite. If you check *The Readers Guide to Periodical*

Literature at your local library, you will find but a single listing on the CFR in over 50 years. And that in the relatively obscure *Atlantic Monthly*. A check of newspaper files shows that only two feature articles on this incredibly powerful organization have appeared, one in the *Christian Science Monitor* and one in the *New York Times*. As we said before, such anonymity can hardly be accidental.

The involvement of the Rockefellers with the media has multi-multi implications. One is that the Rockefeller gang's plans for monopolistic World Government are never, but never, discussed in the machines of mass misinformation. The media decides what the issues will be in the country. They can turn on the poverty issue or turn it off. The same holds true for population explosion, pollution, peace, *detente*, or whatever. We have in this country what columnist Kevin Phillips has termed a mediacracy.

The mediacracy can take a man like Ralph Nader and make him an instant folk hero. Or they can take an enemy of the Rockefellers and create the image that he is a cretin, a buffoon, a bigot, or a dangerous paranoid.

The use of psychology and propaganda, or if you will, brainwashing, is not a Communist invention. It was developed in the West in such places as the Rockefeller-financed Tavistock Institute in England. While the Communists have used these tools for mindbending, so have the Rockefellers. The hidden persuaders from Madison Avenue, the Rand Corp. think-tank or Hudson Institute, can and do manipulate public opinion. The Establishment elitists refer to it as "the engineering of consent." That means we are made to think the manacles they are slipping on our wrists are love bracelets. The techniques developed by the Rockefeller Thought Trust have just been adopted and used more brutally by the Communists.

With money the Rockefellers gained control of the media. With the media the family gained control over public opinion. With control over public opinion they gained control of politics. And with control of politics, they are taking control of the nation.

Chapter Seven
Surrender by Consent

We shall have world government whether or not you like it—by conquest or consent.

CFR member James Warburg
testifying before the Senate Foreign
Relations Committee on February 17, 1950

As we have seen in the preceding chapter, there can be absolutely no doubt that *the* major Rockefeller goal today is the creation of a "New World Order"—a one-world government that would control all of mankind. But, wanting a Global Superstate and getting one are two different things. How do the Rockefellers expect to round up all of us cows and herd us into their World Government corral?

The Rockefellers know that the roads to World Government can be as varied as human hopes, fears, ambitions, ignorance and greed. And since the Rockefellers *never* put all of their financial or political eggs into one basket, you will not be surprised to learn that they are involved in promoting every conceivable route to a World Superstate. If there is an approach they have overlooked, we can't think of it. (And if you can, please don't mention it out loud—or the *New York Times* might announce tomorrow that the Council on Foreign Relations or a Rockefeller Foundation grant is supporting it.)

A complete listing of all organizations, movements, publications, and programs supporting World Government, which in turn are managed behind the scenes by the Rockefeller-CFR axis, would fill a book the size of the Los Angeles area telephone directory. Obviously, we can mention only a few of the more important trails along the Rockefellers' drive toward World Government.

Certainly the most visible pathway toward World Government is the organization that was created in 1945 by the Rockefellers for precisely this purpose—the United Nations. As we shall see in the next chapter, the controlled media have deliberately created a myth that the UN is a meaningless debating society. We are supposed to believe that the Rockefellers have spent millions on an organization that is, at best, an expensive but relatively harmless irritant. This public image of the UN has been invaluable to the global master planners, and it is about as accurate as an itinerant peddler's claim for his sure-fire snake oil potion.

If the Rockefeller thought-controllers can persuade enough Americans to accept voluntarily the surrender of U.S. sovereignty to the United Nations, their long campaign for World Government will be over. The "New World Order" will have arrived—with all the hoopla of a Wall Street ticker tape parade. The Rockefellers would be willing to pay almost any price for such a bloodless *coup d'etat*. In fact, they are paying millions of dollars every year to finance just such a possibility. Here are just a few of the organizations in the United States which are financed and/or directed by the Rockefeller-CFR combine that are actively promoting the voluntary demise of American independence.

American Assembly

American Association for the United Nations

American Friends Service Committee

Arden House Group

Atlantic Union

Business Council

Center for Advanced Study in Behavioral Sciences

Center of Diplomacy and Foreign Policy

Chatham House

Citizens Committee for International Development

Committees on Foreign Relations

Committee for Economic Development

Council on Foreign Relations

Federation of World Governments

Foreign Policy Association

Institute of International Education

Institute for World Order

National Planning Association   U.S. National Commission
The Trilateral Commission   World Affairs Council
United World Federalists

If you recognize more than half of this list, congratulations! You are already well-informed about this Rockefeller road to serfdom. But if most of these names are new to you, we respectfully suggest that you have some homework to do. And while doing it, please remember that some of the most innocent sounding groups, or some apparently ineffective body whose avowed purposes seem totally non-political, may be one of the most dangerous tentacles on the whole World Government octopus.

Such is the case with one of the oldest organizations mentioned above, Atlantic Union. It is the grandaddy of regional government schemes, composed of those who believe that getting half a loaf is half way to getting a whole loaf. Atlantic Unionists argue that regional government is a necessary way station on the road to total World Government. Until Rocky's boy Henry sprung *détente* on them, Atlantic Union was also the organization for one-worlders who claimed to be anti-Communists. (And, indeed, there were some legitimate anti-Communists in the group.)

The Atlantic Unionists believe that our War of Independence was all a ghastly mistake. This may seem a little odd as we prepare to celebrate the nation's bicentennial, but there are as many unreconstructed Tories on Wall Street as there are unreconstructed secessionists in Alabama.

The idea of Atlantic Union had its origin in the fertile brain of an Englishman named Cecil Rhodes, whose dream was to see the United States reannexed to the British Empire. To this end he established the Rhodes Foundation, providing for the education in England of bright young Americans.

In 1939, a Rhodes Scholar named Clarence Streit wrote a book called *Union Now*, which advocated a gradual approach to final world union by way of regional unions, starting with the union between the U.S. and Britain. Committees were set up all over America, and Mr. Streit reported that over two million Americans had signed petitions asking for union with Britain.

In Streit's own words, Atlantic Union, now expanded to include Western Europe, was the first step towards total world government: "It [Union Now] proclaimed the need of world government and insisted that no country needed this more urgently than the United States."

Streit, who has been a close associate of Communists and socialists all his adult life, has no hostility towards collectivism. He said in *Union Now*: "Democracy not only allows mankind to choose freely between capitalism and collectivism, but it includes Marxist governments."

In his pamphlets Streit asks the question: "Does the rise of socialism in some Western European democracies prevent our federating with them?" He answers with an emphatic "No!"

In March 1949, Federal Union set up a political-action unit called the Atlantic Union Committee. The first president of this Committee was former Supreme Court Justice Owen J. Roberts, who said he considers national sovereignty a "silly shibboleth."

More than twenty years ago the *Los Angeles Examiner* described what Atlantic Union would mean to America:

> They [the nations of Western Europe] would impose their socialism in place of our republican self-government, extract taxes from us as they pleased, draft our men for their armies and our women for their factories, appropriate the bulk of our productive wealth for their own enrichment.
>
> How can any Senator or Representative elected to represent the people of the United States bring himself to advocate so clear a policy of national self-destruction?

The goals of Atlantic Union have not changed. But very few newspapers are as courageous or outspoken anymore. Bucking the Rockefellers is *not* the way to build your advertising revenue.

Less than a dozen years after its founding, the Atlantic

Union Committee had grown to 871 wealthy and influential members, 107 of whom were members of the CFR. Today it has some 2,000 members.

An Atlantic Union Resolution which would, in effect, repeal the Declaration of Independence, was first introduced in Congress in 1949. It has been reintroduced every year since, but until recently never received much attention—despite its endorsement by such Rockefeller-CFR stalwarts as Richard Nixon, Hubert Humphrey, George McGovern, Dwight Eisenhower, Adlai Stevenson, John Foster Dulles, Jacob Javits, William Fulbright, Eugene McCarthy, and Henry Kissinger.

In 1975, the Atlantic Union resolution was once more introduced into the House of Representatives. Incredibly, 111 Congressmen (38 more sponsors than the resolution ever had before), all sworn to uphold the Constitution of the United States, officially co-sponsored the measure which would supersede our Constitution! According to the bill's chief sponsor, Illinois Republican Paul Findley:

> This proposal never before had so much vigorous fresh blood as it has today. Nearly half of its sponsors are new—59 to be exact. Of these, 26 are freshmen, elected last November; 13 others voted for it when it was stalled on the floor last year by the thin majority of 210 to 197. Most significant of all, 10 of those who voted against it two years ago and still remain in the House are sponsoring it today; 56 of the 210 who opposed it in 1973 are no longer among the members of the House.

In 1973, the Atlantic Union resolution missed passing by a scant 13 votes. As Findley gloated, many of those who voted against it are now gone and several others who once opposed the measure have seen the Rockefeller handwriting on the wall and have become sponsors.

As you probably suspect, Atlantic Union is a Rockefeller operation.

The Oilbucks Gang has been tied to Atlantic federation for some 35 years. In fact, when Nelson Rockefeller was given the Atlantic Union's highest honor, the Pioneer Award, in 1964, Clarence Streit told the assembled dignitaries at the presentation that Nelson Rockefeller had saved the organization from a dangerous division back in 1939. It seems that the two strongest chapters, one in New York City and the other in Washington, were at loggerheads on where the group's headquarters would be established. Both wanted it in their own city.

Ever the politician, Streit wanted to satisfy both factions, but he didn't have the shekels to finance such an elaborate operation. It was at that moment the Rockefeller cavalry came galloping to the rescue. Nelson promised to provide an entire floor at 10 East 40th Street, New York City, rent free.

Twenty-five years later, it was Rocky's open espousal of ending American independence, expressed in his book *Future of Federalism*, that gave many secret World Government supporters in Congress the courage to speak up. According to Streit:

> "The Future of Federalism" came at a time when other U.S. political leaders and many of our best friends in Congress were afraid even to mention such words as "federal" or "union" in connection with Atlantica, lest they arouse controversy and opposition from misguided "patrioteers."

The Rockefeller family has provided free rental for the Atlantic Union headquarters, and Streit informs us that this fact had been kept a secret for 25 years. Even this admission was made at a private dinner of *Insiders*. You will find no mention of this incredible fact in the newspapers the next day. (Streit's disclosure appeared in their own publication, and was later placed in the *Congressional Record* for all to see by a "misguided patrioteer.") You are not supposed to know that the richest family in the country wants to abolish the independence of the United States.

For those Americans willing to go directly into the Great Merger with the Communists, without shilly-shallying around with regional intermediaries, the Rockefeller-CFR combine has several organizations available to support. The most blatant, as well as the most successful, is probably the United World Federalists. The United World Federalists was formed in 1947 by two CFR stalwarts, Norman Cousins and James P. Warburg (whose statement, promising world government "by consent or conquest," began this chapter). One of the most famous slogans of this Rockefeller front was "One world or none."

The UWF has been particularly effective at appealing to the idealism of youthful Americans, through chapters on many high school and college campuses, with its promise of "world peace through world law." Most of these young members apparently assume that a World Government created and controlled by *Insiders* would protect individual rights, guarantee freedom of the press, respect religious beliefs and practices, and so on. Naturally, the UWF says nothing to disillusion them.

The United World Federalists has been a CFR operation since it was created, more than 25 years ago, by amalgamating three small organizations, the World Federalists, Student Federalists, and Americans United for World Government. Its membership has been heavily interlocked with that of the CFR from the day it began. Yet so successful has been the Rockefeller-CFR public relations job on behalf of the UWF that today it can—and does—promote virtually every major plank of the Communist Party, without losing an ounce of its Establishment-created "respectability."

The first president of the United World Federalists was Cord Meyer Jr., who, of course, was also a member of the CFR. In a very curious book called *Peace or Anarchy*, Meyer touted the usual *Insider* line that the United States should be thrilled to disarm itself and merge into a "Federated World Government" under the control of the United Nations. And here is the kind of "peace" the UWF president wanted to see established:

> . . . once having joined the One-World Federated Government no nation could secede or revolt . . . because with the Atom Bomb in its possession the Federal Government [of the World] would blow that nation off the face of the earth.

Significantly, when he stepped down as UWF president, Meyer slid into a top position with another Rockefeller organization, the Central Intelligence Agency. His activities since then have been cloaked in a veil of secrecy, but one can only assume that his vision of an all-powerful World Government, happily blowing recalcitrant nations "off the face of the earth," has not changed.

In recent decades, UWF* supporters have become much more subtle in their advocacy of a World Superstate. The game is still the same, but the names have been changed—to protect the guilty. They are now selected by Rockefeller's PR boys on Madison Avenue to be much more palatable to the public. You will not, for example, find a UWF member today stating the group's goals quite as crudely as a UWF professor named Milton Mayer did in 1949, when he said: "We must haul down the American flag . . . haul it down, stamp on it, spit on it." The Rockefellers, you understand, never spit; they expectorate.

Although less than one American in a thousand would consider for a moment the suggestion that his political leaders have actually advocated abandoning our independence, the truth is that the UWF has been endorsed by such big-name politicos as Harry Truman, Adlai Stevenson, Hubert Humphrey, Richard Nixon, Jacob Javits, Dwight Eisenhower, Frank Church, Justice William O. Douglas, and Ronald Reagan.

For decades Atlantic Union and United World Federalists and scores of less-effective Rockefeller fronts have followed a course of patient gradualism. They do not expect Americans to accept World Government overnight; like water dripping on a rock, they plan to wear down all opposition in time.

But there are increasing indications that the leaders of

---

*To make their commitment to globalism, not nationalism, even clearer, the UWF changed its name in 1969 to World Federalists, U.S.A.

the conspiratorial internationalists are running out of patience. Sure, they will permit the UWF and assorted schemes to continue on their merry way, urging us to put the gun to our collective heads and pull the trigger—all the while promising us we'll be better off for the experience, of course. But as we shall see in the next chapter, some of the top brass have contingency plans well prepared to move considerably faster should it become necessary.

One development that may signal more severe storms on the horizon was the formation, more than two years ago, of a new entity called "The Trilateral Commission." The founding meeting was called by David Rockefeller, the number one man in the Council on Foreign Relations and Chairman of the Board of Chase Manhattan Bank. When David asks some 200 leading bankers, businessmen, politicians, and labor leaders *throughout the world* to join him in forming a multi-national planning commission, you can be certain that the invitation has all of the force of a royal command.

Long-time Rockefeller watchers know that major shifts in the internationalists' plans are frequently signaled by brief articles in the *New York Times*. So when that *Insiders'* house organ mentioned in a small dispatch on June 18, 1974, that "the lives and fortunes of large numbers of human beings hang upon the outcome of decisions taken by a small handful of national leaders" on the Trilateral Commission, it was time to pay more attention—a lot more attention—to the group. If your life hangs upon (a rather strong choice of words for so august a publication as the *Times*) the deliberations and decisions of this commission, it is time to find out what they are deciding.

The tipoff came with the appointment of Zbigniew Brzezinski as a director of the commission. Shortly after the formation of the Trilateral Commission, the new director (who is an officer of the CFR) wrote an article for the CFR's official journal, *Foreign Affairs*, in which he said:

> The world is not likely to unite [willingly] behind a common ideology or a super-government. The only practical

hope is that it will now respond to a common concern for
its own survival. . . .

. . . . The Atlantic [Union] concept was a creative
response to the problems of the cold war era. Today, the
Atlantic framework is too narrow to encompass the multitude of challenges—and opportunities—that confront the
international community. It is a recognition of this reality
to propose . . . that the active promotion of such trilateral
cooperation must now become the central priority of U.S.
policy.

In other words, Brzezinski says it's time to forget about
the rather open and above-board approach to world
government proposed by Atlantic Union. Voluntary
union will not be achieved in time; it's time to try another
approach. What is that "other approach"? Simply stated,
it is to impose the very same controls over nations that
World Government advocates propose, but this time to do
it under the guise of solving economic, ecological, or
energy problems.

The chairman of The Trilateral Commission is Gerard
C. Smith, another CFR member and former director of the
Arms Control and Disarmament Agency.* Here is how he
describes the purpose of The Trilateral Commission:

The United States, Western Europe, and Japan face a
common condition. They are the major industrial areas of
the world, and they share common concerns about the
problems of environment and modern industrial society.
. . .

They jointly share a global responsibility and *we think
their relations are threatened by domestic concerns* which
tend to drive the regions apart. (Emphasis added.)

According to Smith, the problems each country is fac-

---

*The significance of Smith leaving the Arms Control and Disar-
mament Agency to run this new Rockefeller operation should
not be overlooked. The Disarmament Agency is a key part of
the *Insiders'* program for a World Superstate. (See Chapter
Eight.) For Smith to step down from such a major post means
the Trilateral Commission must *really* be important.

ing may pose a serious obstacle to the establishment of a "New World Order." There is a danger that some nations may become so concerned about solving their own problems (such as having enough fuel to keep their factories going and enough food to feed their citizens), that they will lose sight of the larger objective—building World Government.

The first meeting of David Rockefeller's new group was held in Tokyo on October 21-23, 1973. Sixty-five persons were listed as North American members. Of those, thirty-five are also members of the Council on Foreign Relations.

Six position papers, called "The Triangle Papers," have been issued so far by the Commission: two from the Tokyo meeting in October 1973, three from a meeting in Brussels in June 1974, and one from a Washington, D.C. meeting in December 1974. If the "Triangle Papers" are any indication, we can look for four major thrusts toward world economic controls: The first, toward a "renovated world monetary system"; the second, involving the looting of our resources for the further radicalization of "have-not" nations; the third, toward stepped-up trade with the Communists; and the fourth, toward milking the energy crisis for greater international controls.

So if you've been wondering what the next move of the World Government *Insiders* will be along the road to surrender by consent—they've already made it. The Trilateral Commission has been created by David Rockefeller to guide his fellow internationalists in using their *private* influence to make certain their governments remain on the proper *public* course—a headlong rush toward the Great Merger. And the country that ignores its warnings, and pays too much attention to its "domestic" concerns, may find itself in a food/fuel/financial crisis that will make the Great Depression seem like an idyllic trek through the Promised Land.

THE
UNITED STATES
PROGRAM FOR
FREEDOM GENERAL AND
COMPLETE
FROM DISARMAMENT
WAR PEACEFUL

FREEDOM FROM WAR

THE UNITED STATES PROGRAM FOR GENERAL AND COMPLETE DISARMAMENT IN A PEACEFUL WORLD

* * * *

- The disbanding of all national armed forces and the prohibition of their reestablishment in any form whatsoever other than those required to preserve internal order and for contributions to a United Nations Peace Force;

- The elimination from national arsenals of all armaments, including all weapons of mass destruction and the means for their delivery, other than those required for a United Nations Peace Force and for maintaining internal order;

* * * *

- The U.N. Peace Force, equipped with agreed types and quantities of armaments, would be fully functioning.

- The manufacture of armaments would be prohibited except for those of agreed types and quantities to be used by the U.N. Peace Force and those required to maintain internal order. All other armaments would be destroyed or converted to peaceful purposes.

- The peace-keeping capabilities of the United Nations would be sufficiently strong and the obligations of all states under such arrangements sufficiently far-reaching as to assure peace and the just settlement of differences in a disarmed world.

Chapter Eight
Surrender by Conquest

In Stage III [of disarmament] progressive controlled disarmament . . . would proceed to a point where no state would have the military power to challenge the progressively strengthened UN Peace Force and all international disputes would be settled according to agreed principles of international conduct . . . . The Peace-keeping capabilities of the United Nations would be sufficiently strong and the obligations of all states under such arrangements sufficiently far reaching as to assure peace and the just settlement of differences in a disarmed world.

Department of State
Publication 7277

On his return from Vladivostok, U.S.S.R., where he had signed an agreement drafted at the Strategic Arms Limitation Talks (SALT), President Ford announced in a typically mixed metaphor that he had "put a cap" on the arms race. In the light of previous deals with the Communists, such a pronouncement was incredible. It conjured up memories of Chamberlain, newly arrived from Munich, standing on the sacred ground in which his head was buried and announcing through the sand that the treaty in his hand was proof we would have "peace in our time."

While the Liberal press was singing hosannas to SALT II as the pinnacle of *détente* (French for both a trigger and a lessening of tensions), the Communists were gobbling up territory faster than the Oklahoma Sooners. Using Soviet arms, the Reds were sweeping through Cambodia and South Vietnam. With the planned opening of Suez, they were preparing to link their naval forces in the Mediterranean and the Indian Ocean. And Portugal, a long-time American ally, was being converted into a Soviet outpost in Western Europe. If this is *détente*, bring back the Cold War.

The road toward SALT began at the dawn of the nuclear age, when Leftist scientists and academics, standing at the wailing wall of disarmament, began to bemoan their fear that America's superior nuclear capacity would somehow frighten a worried Soviet Union into launching a major war. The "solution" to this peril begins with the Pugwash Conferences—and might conclude with the forced surrender of a disarmed U.S.

In 1955, the Parliamentary Association for World Government issued a call for a series of "Conferences on Science and World Affairs" between Russian and American scientists and intellectuals. The first of these was held in 1957 at the home of Russophile Cyrus Eaton in Pugwash, Nova Scotia. Eaton, who began his career as secretary to John D. Rockefeller and is now a business partner of the Rockefellers in promoting Red trade, earned the Lenin Peace Prize for fronting the deal and financing the first five Conferences. Since then, more than twenty have been held, most of them outside the United States. All have been financed by the tax-exempt Rockefeller-CFR foundations.

On September 23, 1960, three years after the first Pugwash Conference, the Soviets presented a plan for "total and complete disarmament" to the United Nations. It called for a systematic reduction in arms by major powers of the world. The so-called "Soviet plan" immediately became the beneficiary of extremely influential American support, when a group of powerful proponents of disarmament within the CFR endorsed it.

This was no mere happenstance. A secret CFR disarmament program, entitled "Study No. 7," was made public a few months later. Prepared by the CFR for the Senate Committee on Foreign Relations, "Study No. 7" argued that the United States "must: (1) search for an international order . . . in which many policies are jointly undertaken by . . . states with differing political, economic and social systems, and including states labeling themselves as 'socialist.''' [That is, Communist.] In order to build such a "new international order," the CFR said, we must "maintain and gradually increase the authority of the UN," and "conduct serious negotiations to achieve international agreement on limitation, reduction and control of armaments."*

And here is the amazing part: This CFR position paper had preceded the Soviet proposal of September 23, 1960, by nearly a year. Pugwashed or not, the two schemes were almost identical!

This Pugwash-CFR conspiracy is one of the most brilliant achievements in psychological warfare since the Trojan Horse. While Americans were being told of the horrors of nuclear war and the supposed advantages of limiting our defenses, the Russians were arming to the teeth.

It was in June of 1964 that the Ford Foundation, already famous for bankrolling Rockefeller-approved fascist-socialist causes, put up $325,000 for a Pugwash production called the "Joint U.S.-U.S.S.R. Study Group in Disarmament."

The climate which Rockefeller partner Cyrus Eaton's Pugwash group and the CFR had created was by now well established. Advocates of the New World Order began to crow that World Government was at last in sight.

In September of 1961, the Department of State released Publication 7277, entitled *Freedom From War: The United States Program for General and Complete Disarmament in a Peaceful World*. It was a three-stage program which provided:

> In Stage III progressive controlled disarmament and continuously developing principles and procedures of international law would proceed to a point where no state would have the military power to challenge the progressively strengthened UN Peace Force and all international disputes would be settled according to agreed

---

*Strategy for the Sixties, Jay Cerf and Walter Pozen, New York, Praeger, Inc., 1961.

principles of international conduct. ... The peace-keeping capabilities of the United Nations would be sufficiently strong and the obligations of all states under such arrangements sufficiently far reaching as to assure peace and the just settlement of differences in a disarmed world.

The same month that State Department Publication 7277 was issued, the United States Arms Control and Disarmament Agency was created by Congress. Within forty-eight hours the new Agency presented its disarmament scheme to the United Nations. Naturally, it was a carbon copy of the CFR-Soviet-Pugwash proposals presented to the UN *by the Communists* the year before. While the newspapers and TV have prattled endlessly about disarmament, nary a word has been said about the other side of the coin: all such proposals call for *arming* the United Nations! This apparently is the best-kept secret since the formula for Coca-Cola.

In October of 1968 the U.S. Disarmament Agency issued a revised proposal, entitled *Arms Control and National Security*, which declared:

Since 1959, the agreed ultimate goal of the negotiations has been general and complete disarmament, i.e., the total elimination of all armed forces and armaments except those needed to maintain internal order within states and to furnish the United Nations with peace forces. ... While the reductions were taking place, a UN peace force would be established and developed, and, by the time the plan was completed, it would be so strong that no nation could challenge it.

Notice that the document said, "Since 1959." The U.S. Arms Control and Disarmament Agency was not established until September 1961. But it was in 1959 that the CFR "Study No. 7" was prepared and its contents were transmitted to the Soviets.

How successful have these New World Order disarmers been in implementing their plans? What has happened to our military strength since disarmament was accepted as official U.S. Government policy? The first Secretary of Defense to implement this policy was CFR member

Robert S. McNamara, Secretary of Defense from 1961 through 1968. In *The Betrayers*, Phyllis Schlafly and Chester Ward discuss McNamara's wrecking job. When Robert McNamara left office, they note, he had:

. . . reduced our nuclear striking force by 50% while the Soviets had increased theirs by 300%.

. . . caused the U.S. to lose its lead in nuclear delivery vehicles.

. . . scrapped 3/4 of our multimegaton missiles.

. . . cut back the originally planned 2,000 Minutemen to 1,000.

. . . destroyed all our intermediate and medium-range missiles.

. . . cancelled our 24-megaton bomb.

. . . scrapped 1,455 of 2,710 bombers left over from the Eisenhower Administration.

. . . disarmed 600 of the remaining bombers of their strategic nuclear weapons.

. . . frozen the number of Polaris subs at 41, refusing to build any more missile-firing submarines.

. . . refused to allow development of any new weapons systems except the TFX (F-111).

. . . cancelled Skybolt, Pluto, Dynasoar and Orian [missile systems].

In fact, McNamara destroyed more operational U.S. strategic weapons that the Soviets could have destroyed in a full-scale nuclear attack!

Supporting McNamara's efforts at unilateral disarmament were CFR members John J. McCloy and William C. Foster. McCloy, who preceded David Rockefeller as chairman of the board of both the CFR and the family's piggy bank, Chase Manhattan, was picked by President John F. Kennedy to be chairman of the General Advisory Committee for the Arms Control and Disarmament Agency, a post which he still holds. William C. Foster was appointed director of the Agency. In 1969, Foster was replaced as director by Gerard C. Smith, another CFR member. Smith's successor in 1973 was Fred Ikle, who (this will probably not surprise you) is also a member of the Council on Foreign Relations.

John J. McCloy's current General Advisory Committee is composed of I. W. Abel, Dr. Harold Brown (CFR), William C. Foster (CFR), Kermit Gordon (CFR), Dr. James R. Killian, General Lauris Norstad (CFR), Dr. Jack Ruina (CFR), Dean Rusk (CFR), William Scranton, Dr. John Archibald Wheeler, and, Judith A. Cole, staff director.

What is going on here, alas, is all too simple. The Rockefeller-Establishment *Insiders* of the Council on Foreign Relations are working to weaken America's defensive capacity so the Soviets can "catch up." This policy, they believe, will lead eventually to a merger of political and economic interests—what the CFR calls a New World Order.

This is not academic skylarking. It is, as we have seen, official U.S. policy. The operative phases of this scheme began in earnest when CFR *Insiders* persuaded President Lyndon Johnson to propose the Strategic Arms Limitation Talks (SALT) in 1966. The SALT talks to negotiate a first disarmament treaty were scheduled for July 1968. They were postponed until November 1969 because the Soviets were busy with their invasion of Czechoslovakia—only two weeks after Soviet officials signed the Declaration of Bratislava, guaranteeing Czech independence!

We have made such great progress at SALT that when the first meetings were scheduled in 1968, the Soviets had only 850 long-range missiles while the U.S. had 1,054. But following the seventh SALT meeting, when President Nixon signed accords in Moscow on May 26, 1972, the Soviets had 1,618 ICBMs either deployed or under construction while we, in turn, still had 1,054—the same number as in 1968. This, in short, is the way we have negotiated. We have frozen production and exported U.S. technology to permit the Kremlin first to catch up, and then to surpass us.

What trends must we stop to prevent an ultimatum from the Soviets? To begin with, there is the effort to limit defense spending—especially in the area of strategic weapons development. In the 1974 *Economic Report of the President* we learn that in 1953 our total government spending as a percentage of national income was 33.2 percent. That included 16 percent for domestic spending, including welfare, etc. Twenty years later, in 1973, government spending had risen to 38.6 percent of the national income. During this time the "better Red than dead" boys had cut defense back to 7 percent of the national income while increasing domestic spending to 31.6 percent. You might tap dance through those statistical tulips again. They confirm that the CFR plan is fully operative—that we are being prepared for the New World Order by being collectivized and disarmed at the same time.

Nor do those figures tell the whole story. With the advent of our "professional" Armed Forces, fifty-six percent of the defense budget is now going for *salaries*. Congressman Larry McDonald (D.-Ga.) of the House Armed Services Committee observes:

> The Liberals in Congress are constantly calling for the slashing of the "bloated" Defense budget so they can further increase Welfare spending. Since we cannot cut salaries, about the only thing which can be cut is hardware. Trimming the so-called fat actually turns out to be slicing out bone and muscle. If we had a war, we would have lots of men in uniform, but they wouldn't have adequate equipment with which to fight.

This result is a tribute to the skullduggery and conspiracy of the *Insiders* of the Rockefeller Council on Foreign Relations who planned it that way. Our "military-industrial complex" had to be destroyed to make Soviet "superiority" more plausible. It has, as a result, been literally starved to death on purpose.

Of course all of this was anticipated when President Nixon signed the SALT I agreement in Moscow back in May of 1972. Even the very "Liberal" Senator Henry Jackson (D.Wash.) admitted: "Simply put, the agreement gives the Soviets more of everything: more light ICBMs, more heavy ICBMs, more submarine-launched missiles, more submarines, more payload, even more ABM radars.

In no area covered in the agreement is the United States permitted to maintain parity with the Soviet Union."

It is all too obvious that SALT has not limited the Soviets in any way. The U.S. is being disarmed while the Communists are being given a first-strike Ultimatum Force.*

Remember the steel rolling plants we sold the Soviets on credit? Remember the aluminium factories the Rockefeller-Eaton Axis is building in Eastern Europe? And remember the Kama River truck factory, financed by David Rockefeller's Chase Manhattan Bank, which will be the largest in the world, covering some forty square miles? Truck factories, of course, are where tanks are built.

Now, ask yourself this question: If the Soviets are really sincere about *détente* and peaceful coexistence, why are they arming at such breakneck speed? Why aren't they diverting that spending into desperately needed consumer goods? And why is Henry Kissinger letting them get away with it? The answer is that the Comrades are preparing to deliver the New World Order ultimatum in case Americans refuse to lay down and play dead. In other words, the traps have been set for world government by consent and by conquest.

The Communists are working hand-in-hand with our Establishment *Insiders*. When the former are powerful enough, the latter will insist we must scrap our national sovereignty and merge into a New World Order—our survival will require it!

If we have not the will to resist—to fight for national sovereignty—then we have no deterrent at all. We invite the nuclear ultimatum. And we are, indeed, in grave danger. The last SALT agreement arranged for a "working

---

*The fact that SALT is merely an extension of the 7277 Disarmament Plan was acknowledged in this agreement which stated: *The U.S.A. and the U.S.S.R. regard as the ultimate objective of their efforts the achievement of general and complete disarmament and the establishment of an effective system of international security in accordance with the purposes and principles of the United Nations.*

meeting" between President Ford and Soviet Party Leader Leonid Brezhnev in Vladivostok, November 23 and 24, 1974, after the President had visited Japan and South Korea to make "assurances." As usual, the trusted Dr. Kissinger arrived early to "work out the details." The President dutifully signed what was put in front of him.

The details, as it turned out, limit the U.S. and Soviets to 2,400 land and sea-based missiles and long-range bombers through 1985. The United States, we are told in *Newsweek* for December 9, 1974, has some 2,206 intercontinental missiles (ICBMs), submarine-based missiles (SLBMs), and long-range bombers. The Soviets, we are assured, have *deployed* 2,375 such missiles and bombers. In addition, we agreed to equip only 1,320 missiles with MIRV warheads.

After dispatching Henry Kissinger to Peking to brief the Red Chinese, President Ford returned home to present his version of the summit to twenty-six Congressional leaders. Back in Washington the President crowed: "We put a firm ceiling on the strategic-arms race. What we have done," he stated with a straight face, "is to set firm and equal limits on the strategic forces of each side, thus preventing an arms race ... Vladivostok is a breakthrough for peace . . . future generations will thank us."

The *National Observer* for December 14, 1974, expressed amazement: "With such fanciful descriptions Mr. Ford, he of the plain word and honest face, is beguiling us—or has been beguiled and is merely repeating the phrases the beguilers used on him."

The prestigious *Aviation Week & Space Technology* for December 9, 1974, warned: "The Vladivostok agreement puts a cap on nothing. The new SALT buzzword about 'putting a cap on the arms race' is just some more White House press agentry that would be ludicrous if it had not proved so disastrous to the Nixon Administration and U.S. interests at past summits."

So there you have it. Rockefeller Contingency Plan II— to be used in the event that the American people cannot be persuaded to accept the surrender of U.S. sovereignty to their New World Order—will be the blunt ultimatum: let the UN run the whole show, or those nasty Communists will blast us all to bits.

Step One was a massive media campaign, brainwashing the public into abject horror at the thought of nuclear war.

Step Two was to increase Soviet military muscle (more on this in the next chapter), to lend some credence to Soviet claims of nuclear power.

Step Three was to make certain the U.S. Armed Forces were not permitted to advance technologically. The development of new weapons systems was forbidden; existing armaments were allowed to rust.

Step Four was to win Congressional approval for the Soviet-CFR planned disarmament scheme. What was approved wasn't disarmament at all; it was a proposal to arm a World Government police force by taking weapons from the U.S. and giving them to the UN.

Steps One through Three have already been implemented. And even while you are reading this, *Insiders* in New York, Washington, Geneva, and London are working to convert Step Four from a plan to a fact.

As the CFR's James Warburg declared to the Senate Foreign Relations Committee twenty-five years ago: "We will have world government whether or not you like it—by conquest or consent." Warburg and his fellow conspirators have made certain that whichever deck is used to deal the next hands, the cards have already been stacked against us.

Chapter Nine
Building the Big Red Machine

> *There has been a continuing, albeit concealed, alliance between international political capitalists and international revolutionary socialists—to their mutual benefit.*

> Antony C. Sutton
> *Wall Street And The Bolshevik Revolution*

That the Rockefellers are a unique and remarkable family is an understatement comparable to Custer observing that "the Indians seem restless today" just before his last stand. No fiction written would create such a family. No Hollywood movie mogul could concoct such a group to star in a celluloid epic. The Rockefellers are bigger than life and stranger than fiction.

Yet, while many biographers have told of their fabulous wealth and virtually unlimited economic and political power, few have dealt with the most remarkable aspect of the family—its close relationship over many generations with its supposed arch-enemies, the Communists. Of course, there is much about this strange relationship that we do not know. But what is already a matter of public record is astounding. To say that things are not always what they seem is a hackneyed cliche, but there has never been a mystery to match that of the world Communist movement and the identity of its ultimate backers.

A bit of background is required in order to understand our subject. The Bolshevik Revolution in Russia was obviously one of the great turning points in history. It is an event over which misinformation abounds. The myth-makers and re-writers of history have done their jobs well.

Today, most people believe the Communists were

successful in Russia because they were able to gain the support of peasants who were sick of the tyranny of the Czars. This is not what happened.

While most know that the Bolshevik Revolution took place in November 1917, few recall that the Czar actually abdicated seven months earlier. With the collapse of Czar Nicholas II's monarchy, a provisional government was established by Prince Lvov, who wanted to pattern the new Russian government after the American Republic. But, unfortunately, Lvov was maneuvered out and replaced by Alexander Kerensky, an admitted Marxist who claimed to be an opponent of the Bolsheviks.

At the time the Czar abdicated and for the next several months, the eventual leaders of the Bolshevik Revolution, Lenin and Trotsky, were not even in Russia. Lenin was in Switzerland and had been living in exile since 1905. Trotsky also was in exile, working as a reporter for a Communist newspaper in—would you believe—New York City.

Trotsky was allowed to return to Russia with an American passport; Lenin was spirited across Europe in the famous sealed train. They joined forces and by November, through bribery, cunning, brutality and deception, were able to hire enough thugs and make enough deals to seize control of Petrograd. The Bolsheviks came to power not because the downtrodden masses of Russia called them *back*, but because very powerful men in Europe and the United States, including members of the Rockefeller family, *sent them in*.

But while these facts have been somewhat suppressed, the biggest secret of all is that throughout this period, the financing for the revolution came from super capitalists in the West, and primarily from the United States.

A meticulously documented book on this subject was written by Antony Sutton, a research fellow for the prestigious Hoover Institution for War, Revolution and Peace at Stanford University. Entitled *Wall Street And The Bolshevik Revolution*, this book by a respected and fastidiously thorough scholar was almost universally ignored by the mass media. One does not have to be a Quiz Kid to figure out why. Sutton sets the stage for the Bolshevik Revolution with this background:

> . . . While monopoly control of industries was once the objective of J. P. Morgan and J. D. Rockefeller, by the late nineteenth century the inner sanctums of Wall Street understood that the most efficient way to gain an unchallenged monopoly was to "go political" and make society go to work for the monopolists—under the name of the public good and the public interest. This strategy was detailed in 1906 by Frederick C. Howe in his *Confessions of a Monopolist*. Howe, by the way, is also a figure in the story of the Bolshevik Revolution.

In his book Howe had stated:

> These are the rules of big business. They have super-seded the teachings of our parents and are reducible to a simple maxim: Get a monoply; let Society work for you; and remember that the best of all business is politics, for a legislative grant, franchise, subsidy or tax exemption is worth more than a Kimberly or Comstock lode, since it does not require any labor, either mental or physical, for its exploitation.

Sutton postulates why wealthy men like the Rocke-fellers would cooperate with and even finance the very Communists who are allegedly sworn to bury them. The British-born scholar points out:

> . . . one barrier to mature understanding of recent history is the notion that all capitalists are the bitter and unswerving enemies of all Marxists and Socialists. This erroneous idea originated with Karl Marx and was un-doubtedly useful to his purposes. In fact, the idea is non-sense. There has been a continuing, albeit concealed, alliance between international political capitalists and international revolutionary socialists—to their mutual benefit.

Through Sutton we can learn the names of the secret men who bankrolled the conspiracy in Russia. We know that no revolution can be successful without organization and money. The "downtrodden masses" usually provide

little of the former and none of the latter. But the Rocke-
fellers and their cohorts can provide both. In *The
Surrender of An Empire*, the brilliant English historian
Nesta Webster observed:

> Had the Bolsheviks been, as they are frequently
> represented, a mere gang of revolutionaries out to destroy
> property, first in Russia, and then in every other country,
> they would naturally have found themselves up against
> organized resistance by the owners of property all over the
> world, and the Moscow blaze would have been rapidly ex-
> tinguished. It was only owing to the powerful influences
> behind them that this minority party was able to seize the
> reins of power and, having seized them, to retain their hold
> of them up to the present day.

Sutton introduces his evidence of "powerful
influences" behind the Communists by stating:

> In brief, this is a story of the Bolshevik Revolution and
> its aftermath, but a story that departs from the usual con-
> ceptual straitjacket approach of capitalists versus Com-
> munists. Our story postulates a partnership between inter-
> national monopoly capitalism and international revo-
> lutionary socialism for their mutual benefit. The final
> human cost of this alliance has fallen upon the shoulders
> of the individual Russian and the individual American.
> Entrepreneurship has been brought into disrepute and the
> world has been propelled toward inefficient socialist
> planning as a result of these monopoly maneuverings in
> the world of politics and revolution . . .
>
> So long as we see all international revolutionaries and all
> international capitalists as implacable enemies of one
> another, then we miss a crucial point—that there has
> indeed been some operational cooperation between inter-
> national capitalists, including fascists.

Sutton then proceeds to present evidence of such
cooperation. The proofs—which are on the public record—
that international banking elements, most notably Morgan
and Rockefeller interests, financed the take-over by the
Bolsheviks, are simply overwhelming. The thousands of
facts and documents that Sutton cites are too numerous to
even summarize here. For those interested in the complete

story, I highly recommend reading Sutton's book, *Wall Street And The Bolshevik Revolution*.

The Hoover Institute researcher asks the obvious question: What is the motivation behind this coalition of capitalists and Bolsheviks? The advantages to the Communists are obvious. But of what possible benefit could such a union be to the super-capitalists of the West?

Sutton suggests that Russia was then—and is today—the largest untapped market in the world. Moreover, Russia, then and now, comprises the greatest potential competitive threat to American industrial and financial supremacy. "Wall Street," says Sutton, "must have cold shivers when it visualizes Russia as a second super American industrial giant." By saddling Russia with an unproductive economic system dependent on the West for continuous infusions of capital and technology for survival, Russia could be both exploited and contained. Sutton concludes:

> Revolution and international finance are not at all inconsistent if the result of revolution is to establish more centralized authority. International finance prefers to deal with central governments. The last thing the banking community wants is laissez-faire economy and decentralized power because these would disperse power.

> This, therefore, is an explanation that fits the evidence. This handful of bankers and promoters was not Bolshevik, or Communist, or socialist, or Democrat, or even American. Above all else these men wanted markets, preferably captive international markets—and a monopoly of the captive world market as the ultimate goal. . . .

> Wall Street did indeed achieve its goal. American firms controlled by this syndicate were later to go on and build the Soviet Union, and today are well on their way to bringing the Soviet military-industrial complex into the age of the computer.

Of course, far more is involved here than just monopolists seeking new captive markets. The same people who bankrolled the Russian Communist Revolution turn out to be the same ones who fastened the Marxist graduated income tax onto the American middle-class while avoiding it themselves; and it is the same group that foisted the fraudulent Federal Reserve System onto an unsuspecting American public. The actions of these super-capitalists over a period of many decades reveal that they were not merely plotting to acquire more profits; they were involved in a conspiracy for control of the world!

No doubt all this has been a handy and profitable by-product of the super-capitalist capture of Russia. But, it is only part of a bigger picture. Like the cartel capitalists, the Communists work for a world government. And world government is promoted from both the top and the bottom of the conspiratorial apparatus.

In the Bolshevik Revolution we have some of the world's richest and most powerful men financing a movement which claims that its very reason for existence is to strip of their wealth such super-rich cartel and banker capitalists as the Rockefellers.

But obviously these men have no fear of international Communism. It is only logical to assume that if they financed it, and are willing—even eager—to cooperate with it, it must be because they control it. Can there be any other explanation that makes sense? Remember that for over 100 years it has been a standard operating procedure of the Rockefellers and their allies to control both sides of every conflict.

Having created their colony in Russia, the Rockefellers and their allies have struggled mightily ever since to keep it alive. Beginning in 1918 this clique has been engaged in transferring money and, probably more important, technical information to the Soviet Union. This is made abundantly clear in Antony Sutton's monumental three-volume history, *Western Technology and Soviet Economic Development*. Using for the most part official State Department documents, Sutton proves beyond any possible doubt that virtually everything the Soviets possess has been acquired from the West, principally America. It is not an exaggeration to say that the USSR was made in the USA. No one has even attempted to refute Sutton's almost excessively scholarly works. They can't. But the misinformation machines that compose our mediacracy can ignore Sutton. And they do. Totally.

None of the foregoing makes sense if Communism really is what the Communists and the Rockefeller Establishment tell us it is. But if Communism is an arm of a bigger conspiracy to control the world by power-mad billionaires (and brilliant but ruthless academicians who have shown them how to use their power) it all becomes perfectly logical.

It is at this point that we should again make it clear that this conspiracy is not made up solely of Rockefellers and other bankers and international cartelists, but includes every field of human endeavor. Starting with Voltaire and Adam Weishaupt and running through John Ruskin, Sidney Webb, Nicholas Murray Butler, and on to the present with *Insiders* such as Henry Kissinger and John Kenneth Galbraith, it has always been the scholar looking for avenues of power who has shown the "sons of the very powerful" how their wealth could be used to rule the world.

We cannot stress too greatly the importance of the reader keeping in mind that this book is discussing only one segment of the conspiracy. Other important segments which work to foment labor, religious and racial strife in order to promote socialism have been described in numerous other books. These other divisions of the conspiracy often operate independently of the Rockefellers and other international bankers and it would certainly be disastrous to ignore the danger to our freedom they represent.

It would be equally disastrous to lump all businessmen and bankers into the conspiracy. A distinction must be drawn between competitive free enterprise, the most moral and productive system ever devised, and cartel capitalism dominated by industrial monopolists and international bankers. The difference is crucial: the private enterpriser operates by offering products and services in a competitive free market, where consumers have numerous choices offered to them, while cartel capitalists use the government to force the public to do business with them. These corporate socialist-fascists are the deadly enemies of competitive private enterprise.

Liberals are willing to believe that the Rockefellers will fix prices, rig markets, establish monopolies, buy politicians, exploit employees and fire them the day before they are eligible for pensions, but they absolutely will not believe that these same men would want to rule the world or would use Communism as the striking edge of their conspiracy. When one discusses the machinations of the Rockefellers and their allies, Liberals usually respond by saying "But don't you think they mean well?"

However, if you assemble the evidence, carefully present your proofs, and try to expose these power seekers, the Establishment's mass media will accuse you of being a dangerous paranoid who is "dividing" our people. In every other area, of course, they encourage dissent as being healthy in a "democracy."

The Rockefeller-CFR *Insiders* began pushing to open up Communist Russia to U.S. traders soon after the revolution. However, at that time public opinion ran so high against the Bolsheviks because of their barbarism that it was official U.S. government policy not to deal with the outlaw government. The U.S. did not even recognize the Bolshevik regime until 1933.

Galloping to the rescue were the super-capitalists of the West—men like the Vanderlips, the Harrimans, and the Rockefellers. One of the first to arrive was Frank Vanderlip, an agent of the Rockefellers and president of the Rockefeller First National City Bank, who once favorably compared Lenin to George Washington.

Before the Bolshevik revolt, Russia had succeeded the U.S. as the world's number one oil producer. The chaos and destruction of the revolution effectively eliminated Standard Oil's competition from Russia for several years— until Standard could move in and get a piece of the Russian oil business.

In 1926, Standard Oil of New York and its subsidiary, Vacuum Oil Company, concluded a deal to market Soviet oil in European countries. Part of the price for the arrangement, it was reported at the time, was a loan of $75,000,000 to the Bolsheviks. In 1927, Russia's secret partner, Standard Oil of New York, built an oil refinery in Russia. The refinery helped immeasurably in putting the Bolshevik economy back on its feet. According to Professor Sutton, "This was the first United States investment in Russia since the Revolution." (We have been unable to find out if Standard Oil was even theoretically expropriated by the Communists.)

It is possible the Rockefellers still own oil production facilities behind the Iron Curtain and get the profits out through Switzerland. By doing this, they would not have to share the loot with stockholders or the tax collector.

Wherever Standard Oil would go, Chase National Bank was sure to follow. In order to rescue the Bolsheviks, who were supposedly the archenemy of profit-seeking businessmen, the Chase National Bank was instrumental in establishing the American-Russian Chamber of Commerce in 1922. President of the Chamber was Reeve Schley, a vice-president of Chase National Bank. According to Professor Sutton:

> In 1925, negotiations between Chase and Prom-bank extended beyond the finance of raw materials and mapped out a complete program for financing Soviet raw material exports to the U.S. and imports of U.S. cotton and machinery . . . Chase National Bank and the Equitable Trust Company were leaders in the Soviet credit business.

The Rockefeller's Chase National Bank also was involved in selling Bolshevik bonds in the United States in 1928. Patriotic organizations denounced the Chase as an "international fence." Chase was called "a disgrace to America . . . They will go to any lengths for a few dollars' profits."

Congressman Louis McFadden, chairman of the House Banking Committee, maintained in a speech to his fellow Congressmen:

The Soviet government has been given United States Treasury funds by the Federal Reserve Board and the Federal Reserve Banks acting through the Chase Bank and the Guaranty Trust Company and other banks in New York City . . .

. . . Open up the books of Amtorg, the trading organization of the Soviet government in New York, and of Gostorg, the general office of the Soviet Trade Organization, and of the State Bank of the Union of Soviet Socialist Republics and you will be staggered to see how much American money has been taken from the United States Treasury for the benefit of Russia. Find out what business has been transacted for the State Bank of Soviet Russia by its correspondent, the Chase Bank of New York;
. . .

In his three-volume history of Soviet technological development, Professor Sutton proves conclusively that there is hardly a segment of the Soviet economy which is not a result of the transference of Western, particularly American, technology.

This cannot be wholly the result of accident. For fifty years the Federal Reserve-CFR-Rockefeller-*Insider* crowd has advocated and carried out policies aimed at increasing the power of their satellite, the Soviet Union. Meanwhile, America spends $90 billion a year on defense to protect itself from the enemy the *Insiders* are building up.

What has been true in the past is even more valid today. Heading the parade to transfer technology and increase aid and trade with the Communists are the Rockefellers and the Council on Foreign Relations.

The bandmaster for the entire enterprise is David Rockefeller.

Most Americans regard Nelson Rockefeller as the most important member of the Rockefeller family. He is, after all, the (unelected) Vice President of the United States. Since 1960 he has been a perennial candidate for the Presidency. Nelson Rockefeller is a compulsive extrovert who loves to be in the public eye. As a result, he is far better known than his brothers. But notoriety is an unreliable measure of power.

Students of the Eastern Establishment are well aware that while Nelson gets the ink, it is little brother David who wields the power. "As the *de facto* head of the American Establishment," reports *Time*, "It has been said that for him the presidency would be a demotion." The *New York Times* concurs: "He has come to be regarded as a spokesman for enlightened American capitalism." Of course, to the *New York Times*, "enlightened American capitalism" means government planning of virtually every facet of the American economy, major transfers of America's vital technology to the Communists, the internationalizing of American business through multinational holding companies, and the creation of a World Government.

In 1964 David Rockefeller and Nikita Khrushchev were closeted in Moscow for two and a half hours. The *Chicago Tribune* of September 12, 1964, reported:

> David Rockefeller . . . briefed President Johnson today on his recent meeting with Premier Nikita S. Khrushchev of Russia . . . the Red leader said the United States and the Soviet Union "should do more trade." Khrushchev, according to Rockefeller, said he would like to see the United States extend long-term credits to the Russians.

As a matter of fact, the meeting between Rockefeller and Khrushchev had been held two months earlier, in July. Apparently whatever trouble had developed was not settled until the President was briefed in September. Within a month, Khrushchev was deposed. David Rockefeller was soon meeting on the Black Sea with his successor, and in October of 1966 L.B.J. announced his new policy of "building bridges" to Eastern Europe. This was at the time the Communists were escalating the Vietnam War, and virtually all of the war materiél to do so came from the munitions factories of Eastern Europe. It seemed politically incredible for Johnson to propose such a policy while American troops were being killed and maimed by ammunition and weapons from the Communist bloc. It *would* have been flabbergasting if one had not been following the machinations of David Rockefeller.

On October 7, 1966, President Johnson, a man who had appointed a CFR member to virtually every strategic position in his administration, stated:

> We intend to press for legislative authority to negotiate trade agreements which could extend most-favored-nation tariff treatment to European Communist states . . .
>
> We will reduce export controls on East-West trade with respect to hundreds of non-strategic items . . .

Six days later, the *New York Times* reported:

> The United States put into effect today one of President Johnson's proposals for stimulating East-West trade by removing restrictions on the export of more than four hundred commodities to the Soviet Union and Eastern Europe . . .
>
> Among the categories from which items have been selected for export relaxation are vegetables, cereals, fodder, hides, crude and manufactured rubber, pulp and waste paper, textiles and textile fibers, crude fertilizers, metal ores and scrap, petroleum, gas and derivitives, chemical compounds and products, dyes, medicines, fireworks, detergents, plastic materials, metal products and machinery, and scientific and professional instruments.

Virtually every one of these "non-strategic" items has a direct or indirect use in war. Later, items such as rifle cleaning compounds, electronic equipment, computers, and radar were declared "non-strategic" and cleared for shipment to the Soviet Union. Congress drew the lines at sending "strategic" goods to the Reds, but the trick was simply to declare almost everything "non-strategic." A machine gun is strategic, but the tools for making it and the chemicals to propel the bullets were declared "non-strategic."

The Viet Cong and North Vietnamese received 85 percent of their war materials from Russia and the Soviet-bloc nations. Since their economies are incapable of supporting a war, the Communist arm of the conspiracy needed help from the Finance Capitalist arm. The United States financed and equipped both sides of the terrible Vietnamese war, killing nearly 55,000 of our own soldiers by proxy. Again, the mass media kept the American public from learning this shocking truth.

Not surprisingly, the Rockefellers have been leaders in championing this bloody trade. On January 16, 1967, one of the most incredible articles ever to appear in a newspaper graced the front page of the Establishment's daily, the *New York Times*. Under the headline, "Eaton Joins Rockefellers To Spur Trade With Reds," the article stated:

> An alliance of family fortunes linking Wall Street and the Midwest is going to try to build economic bridges between the free world and Communist Europe.
>
> The International Basic Economy Corporation, controlled by the Rockefeller brothers, and Tower International, Inc., headed by Cyrus S. Eaton, Jr., Cleveland financier, plan to cooperate in promoting trade between the Iron Curtain countries, including the Soviet Union ...

International Basic Economy Corporation (IBEC) is run by Richard Aldrich, grandson of Federal Reserve plotter Nelson Aldrich, and Rodman Rockefeller (CFR), Rocky's son. On October 20, 1969, IBEC announced that N. M. Rothschild & Sons of London had entered into partnership with the firm.

Cyrus Eaton, Jr. is the son of the notoriously pro-Soviet Cyrus Eaton, who began his career as secretary to John D. Rockefeller. It is believed that Eaton's rise to power in finance resulted from backing by his mentor. So the agreement between Tower International and IBEC continues an old alliance. Although Eaton's name does not appear on the CFR's membership rolls, the Reece Committee which investigated foundations for Congress in 1953 found that the notorious Soviet apologist was a secret member.

Among the "non-strategic" items which the Rockefeller-Eaton axis is going to build for the Communists are ten rubber goods plants and a $50 million aluminum-producing plant for the Reds. (Aluminum for jet planes has been considered "non-strategic" under the Johnson-Nixon-Ford Administrations.)

Even more incredibly, the *Times* reveals:

> Last month, Tower International reached a tentative

New York Times   January 16, 1967

Eaton Joins Rockefellers To Spur Trade With Reds

Cleveland and New York Financiers to Set Up an East-West Exchange

By ROBERT E. BEDINGFIELD

An alliance of family fortunes linking Wall Street and the Midwest is going to try to build economic bridges between the free world and Communist Europe.

The International Basic Economy Corporation, controlled by the Rockefeller brothers, and Tower International, Inc., headed by Cyrus S. Eaton Jr., Cleveland financier, plan to cooperate in promoting trade between the Iron Curtain countries, including the Soviet Union, and the United States, Canada and Latin America.

The I.B.E.C. was organized in 1947 under the principal direction of Nelson A. Rockefeller, now New York's Governor. It was organized as an investment company specializing in enterprises in underdeveloped nations. The company already has interests in 20 foreign countries,

Cyrus S. Eaton Jr.

but none is in the Communist bloc.

Tower International is a wholly owned subsidiary of Tower Industries, a partnership

Continued on Page 67, Column 1

David Rockefeller, chairman of the Chase Manhattan Bank, is the most important and most effective promoter in the U.S. of aid to the Communists. He was all smiles (above) after concluding a deal in Red China with Chou En-lai; he has joined with Cyrus Eaton Jr. (see clipping at left) to promote further trade with the Soviet Union; his successes have delighted such important Communist rulers as Soviet Finance Minister V. F. Garbuzov, (below). Thanks to the House of Rockefeller, "trade" with the Communists (always financed by the U.S. taxpayer, of course), now amounts to millions of dollars every year.

agreement with the Soviet patent and licensing organization. Licensintorg, covering future licensing and patent transactions. Until now, Mr. Eaton said, the Russians have left the buying and selling of licenses and patents to the Amtorg Trading Corporation, the official Soviet agency in this country for promoting Soviet-American trade.

This means that the Rockefellers and Eatons have a monopoly on the transfer of technological capability to the supposed enemies of the super-rich, the Soviet Union. According to the *Times*:

Mr. Eaton acknowledged the difficulties that Amtorg's representatives had encountered here in trying to arrange licensing agreements with American companies. "As you can imagine," he said, "it is almost impossible for a Russian to walk into the research department of an American aerospace company and try to arrange the purchase of a patent."

Certainly every loyal American will say to himself, "Well, I would hope to God the Soviets couldn't walk into our defense plants and buy a patent." The Rockefellers and the Eatons have solved that problem for the Communists. Now, instead of dealing with an official agency of the Soviet government, American concerns will be dealing with the Rockefellers. You can imagine how many doors that will open to the Communists!

Thus, by the purchase of patents for the Communists, the Rockefellers are virtually in charge of research and development for the Soviet military machine. Their goal is to enable the Soviets to mass-produce American developments. And let us emphasize that the transfer of such technical knowledge is even more important than the sale of weapons. Ammunition is used once, then it is gone. Weapons break down, vehicles need replacement parts, and sophisticated arms are not easy to produce in a backward economy, no matter how much manpower is available.

While the trade doors were opened during the LBJ Administration, the advent of *détente* under the Nixon-Kissinger era produced an open house in American plants and research labs for the Red traders. Now, a process that may have taken an American corporation a decade to develop is transferred *in toto* to the Communists. Does it make sense to spend $90 billion a year on national defense and then deliberately to increase the war-making potential of an avowed enemy? It does to Mr. Rockefeller and the *Insiders*.

Since the Rockefellers now have an exclusive contract to supply American patents to the Soviets, they are by dictionary definition agents of the Big Red Machine. It goes without saying that they are the most important Communist agents in history. Or perhaps it would be more accurate to define the Communists as Rockefeller agents?

An increasingly important tool for the looting of America by the Rockefellers and their cohorts is the Export-Import Bank, known as Eximbank. It was established in 1934 to finance and promote trade with the Soviet Union. But it wasn't until Richard Nixon signed a "Presidential Determination" on October 18, 1972, that the Eximbank began to finance trade with the Soviets.

The process by which the Eximbank works is simple enough. A U.S. exporter goes to his own bank, which makes arrangements for the Eximbank to loan money to the exporter's foreign buyer. Eximbank then grants a credit to the American bank, which in turn pays the U.S. exporter. Thus the exporter is immediately paid, the American bank is cut in on the deal, and the foreign importer gets a subsidized interest rate.

Who pays the interest subsidy? You hardly need ask. The U.S. taxpayer pays it through Treasury grants to the Eximbank. While most Americans consider themselves lucky if they can arrange to borrow money for less than twelve percent interest, and even the prime rate (the rate at which the largest American corporations with the best credit rating can borrow) is as high as ten percent, the Eximbank has been making loans to foreigners at six percent interest. The difference is a four percent subsidy to any foreigner who buys our goods.

What happens if the foreign buyer defaults? Auf

Wiedersehen. Adios. Sayonara. If the customer sneaks out of the restaurant without paying the check, the waiter puts the arm on the American taxpayer who, once again, picks up the tab. How would you like to be in a business in which the government paid you in full for all sales and accepted the responsibility for collecting all accounts receivable? As the late General Thomas Lane noted:

> In this system, the U.S. exporter has nothing to lose by sales to bad credit risks. The U.S. commercial bank has nothing to lose. The inclination therefore under our profit system is to sell products to anyone who will sign a loan agreement which you can run by the Eximbank. Irresponsibility is rewarded . . .
>
> It is an old story. Public money is nobody's money. As a sense of civic responsibility declines, the public money is used to private advantage [often the Rockefellers].

As with other free enterprisers, we favor foreign trade. But when American exporters ask the taxpayers to take the risks while they take a guaranteed profit, it is not trade but looting. It is as though you were an automobile dealer with an exclusive to sell Cadillacs to deadbeats in Chad, and you had a guarantee that American taxpayers would make all payments the Chads defaulted. Assuredly, you could "sell" a lot of cars that way. You could unload every Cadillac General Motors could produce! And you wouldn't care a fig whether the *customer* ever pays for the car.

Shortly after the May 1972 Summit Conference in Moscow, the Nixon Administration began pushing to extend the credit of the U.S. taxpayers directly to the Soviets. As part of the Nixon-Kissinger *detente*, Congress was to extend to the Bolsheviks tariff status as a "Most Favored Nation," and Eximbank loans were to be arranged for the transfer of the most advanced American technology to Russia and for the development of Soviet energy sources. A UPI release dated July 17, 1973, provides the explanation David Rockefeller gave for such outrages:

David Rockefeller, board chairman of Chase Manhattan

Bank, urged Congress Tuesday to grant most favored nation trading status to the Soviet Union, claiming the move could help slow the arms race. "The desire of the Soviets to use Western trade, credits and technology to bolster their own economy hopefully could be accompanied by their giving lower priority to military programs," Rockefeller testified . . . "We haven't stopped the arms race by withholding exports (in the past)," he said.

David told an audience in Rome that he would replace the Iron Curtain with "a plate-glass curtain." He claimed: "Better communication and then understanding through expanding trade are ingredients of world peace." Just as the scrap metal we sold Japan before Pearl Harbor helped bring peace!

So far, Most Favored Nation status has not been granted by Congress because of publicity about Russia's policy of refusing emigration by Soviet Jews to Israel. But the sluice gates for loans have been opened. Already a legal counselor for Eximbank, under pressure from President Nixon and Secretary of State Henry Kissinger, has pushed the bank's directors to approve questionable loans to the Reds.

As part of the massive effort to build the Communist economy by looting the United States, *on credit*, Richard Nixon appointed William Casey as president of the Export-Import Bank. Casey, a member of the Rocke-feller-controlled CFR, is the perfect man for the job that Kissinger and the Rockefellers have in mind. As part of his goal of promoting "trade" with the Communists, last year he told the Society of American Business Writers:

> To implement this vital aspect of our overall foreign policy, our Ambassadors to Communist nations have been instructed to put trade promotion at the top of their list of priorities. Shortly we will have doubled the number of State Department employees serving in commercial positions in the U.S.S.R., eastern Europe and [Communist] China.

Naturally the Communists are delighted to have the

American super-capitalists build factories for them as long as the American taxpayers agree to pick up the tab when the Commissars default. It is foreign aid in a big, big way!

The first of the giant projects we are inflating our currency to build on credit for our Bolshevik brothers is the Kama River factory, which is to be the largest producer of trucks in the world. But please don't mention that trucks are the backbone of modern military operations, and that during open warfare truck factories are quickly converted to build tanks. If you do so, Liberals will look at you as if you have four heads and nine eyes.

The Kama River factory will produce 150,000 heavy trucks and 150,000 heavy engines per year. This output is greater than the *combined* production of such trucks by all factories in the United States. The complex is being built by a division of the Pullman Company at a cost of two billion dollars. The Soviets are going to put up ten percent of the cash for the project, while David Rockefeller's Chase Manhattan Bank and the Export-Import Bank will each advance forty-five percent.

To say that Eximbank is bending over backwards with our tax dollars to accommodate the Soviets is like saying that J. Paul Getty is fairly confident his personal cheque won't bounce. On Exim's usual loans, repayments must start in three to five or, at the most, seven years. The repayment period for *this* loan is twelve years, with a grace period of 4.5 years. Which means that it will be 16.5 years, if ever, before anyone sees the first payment! Try to get that kind of a deal as an American businessman . . . at six percent interest.

And what happens when the Comrades don't pay? Do we foreclose and repossess the factory? That's about as practical as growing bananas in Minnesota. Krupp, the German industrial giant, almost collapsed as a result of its extension of credit to the Soviets. It had to be bailed out by its government.

But, you say, surely David Rockefeller, the shrewdest and most powerful banker in the world, would not risk Chase Manhattan's money unless he were sure of repayment. You're right. David *is* sure of repayment. Chase's loan is guaranteed by the U.S. taxpayer through other government agencies, the Overseas Private Investment Corporation and the Foreign Credit Insurance Association. The U.S. taxpayer is on the hook for every dime. Just as with the Eximbank loans, OPIC and FCIA guarantee the "businessmen" a profit no matter how badly the deal turns out. What is happening is that we are *giving* the Soviets a two-billion-dollar truck plant, and insuring the Rockefellers' cut on the deal.

The Kama River project kicked off a spree of such looting. One of these loans is for thirty-six million dollars to help construct and equip an international trade center in Moscow. Joint venturing in this deal—all fully guaranteed by you, the taxpayer—are Chase Manhattan and the Bank of America. Arranged by Armand Hammer of Occidental Petroleum, a personal friend of Lenin and son of a founder of the U.S. Communist Party, the huge Trade Center will be built by the Bechtel Corporation. Comrade Hammer and his Occidental Petroleum also have a huge natural gas deal in the mill with the Soviets. According to former Eximbank boss Henry Kearns:

> For a proposed gas development deal in Siberia that the Soviets are eager to make, the required Eximbank credit is $1.5 billion — more than the bank has granted any other customer. The Soviet Union has already received Exim credits of about $350 million without disclosing financial data . . .

The Nixon-Kissinger Administration had to pour millions in paper currency into our economy, thus pushing inflation higher, to lend the Soviet Union $180 million at six percent interest. The deal is for the construction on a Soviet site of a new fertilizer plant made in the U.S.A. This, incidentally, comes at a time when America is in the midst of a severe fertilizer shortage. Crops are being limited in our own country because of that shortage, but our government is determined to help the Comrades at our expense, by looting us of the hardware to build this desperately needed fertilizer plant.

The cost of the Russian fertilizer plant will be $400 million. Of this, the Soviet Union is putting up only $40 million—a mere 10 percent of the cost. All the rest will come from the U.S.

In addition to the Export-Import Bank's loan, for which the bank has already made a preliminary commitment, private American banks will lend another $180 million for the Russian plant—but at a realistic 10 to 12 percent interest. The American taxpayer is therefore subsidizing the Export-Import Bank's part of the loan—a subsidy that could cost between $50 million and $75 million in lost interest over the 12-year period of the loan.

"The Soviet Union is the last great undeveloped market for the U.S.," says Alfred R. Wentworth, senior vice president of Chase Manhattan Bank and head of Chase's recently opened Moscow office. "It now is opening up, and our bank wants to participate in the many opportunities being created."

To be sure no one misunderstands, Chase Manhattan Bank has been running advertisements in major newspapers across the country. They read: "Now you can get banking insights on developing business relationships in the Soviet Union direct from our Moscow office . . . In addition to our Moscow office, we have another in Vienna for dealings in Eastern Europe . . . Our Moscow representatives can be contacted at: Metropol Hotel, 1 Karl Marx Square, Room 227, Moscow, USSR. Tel: 225-6277. From 1 Chase Manhattan Plaza to 1 Karl Marx Square, we're international money experts with a knack for making good sense out of confusing East-West trade talk."

One would expect the Rockefellers to open up shop at the most prestigious (and, as *Business Week* says, "symbolic") address in town. As *Newsweek* magazine headlined its report: The Kremlin now has a "Comrade at Chase."

So has Peking. After David and Nelson Rockefeller called for the "normalizing of relations" and establishing "trade" with Mao Tse-tung and the Red Chinese, Richard Nixon and Henry Kissinger reversed the Republican platform and a hundred Nixon promises to follow that line also. The door was opened for trade with the butchers of Red China.

While Mr. Nixon's sudden cozying up to the Peking mob received reams of comment and publicity, there is one aspect of all this which has attracted virtually no attention. It is the fact that large oil deposits have been found near the Senkaka Islands in the East China Sea.

Our *Insider*-arranged deals with Red China are cut from the same cloth as our "trade" with the Soviet bloc; we have made numerous concessions and have asked none in return. Perhaps one of the concessions "we" will receive will be drilling rights for Standard Oil. After all, David Rockefeller has been promoting an opening with Red China for the past five years. Yes, the plot thickens. And in this case oil is thicker than blood.

"I'm very encouraged," said David Rockefeller in July 1973. "In every case we've been invited by the socialist governments and have been warmly and generously received even though I head a large capitalist bank and my name is closely identified with capitalism."

David was so impressed with the glories of Maoland that he wrote a puff piece for the *New York Times* of August 10, 1973, entitled "From A China Traveler." The chairman of the Council on Foreign Relations observed:

> One is impressed immediately by the sense of national harmony . . . Whatever the price of the Chinese Revolution, it has obviously succeeded not only in producing a more efficient and dedicated administration but also in fostering high morale and community of purpose . . . The social experiment in China under Chairman Mao's leadership is one of the most important and successful in human history.

Batten, Barton, Dursten & Osborne couldn't have written better ad copy to puff the "social experiment" which has killed some sixty-four million of its own people and keeps millions more in the slavery of labor camps.

"And you must remember," says David Rockefeller,

"the Chinese are not only purposeful and intelligent, they also have a large pool of cheap labor. So they should be able to find ways to get trading capital." If wages are low behind the Iron Curtain in Europe, imagine how attractive they are in Red China. Such things are not missed by David Rockefeller.

What does the building of the Big Red Machine in the Soviet Union and Red China mean? Constructing some of the world's largest factories for the Soviet Union, and shipping the Communists the most sophisticated U.S. technology and equipment, has a multitude of implications. Professor Antony Sutton, the world's foremost expert on the use of Western technology to develop the Soviet Union, has written an entire book on this subject under the provocative but very deliberate title, *National Suicide*.

The military potential of the industrial plants which we are building for the Soviets should be obvious to anyone. Trucks, aircraft, oil, steel, petro-chemicals, aluminum, computers—these are the very sinews of a military-industrial complex. These factories, the product of American genius and financed by American capital, could have been built in the United States. Instead, they are constructed at the U.S. taxpayers' expense in the Soviet Union—a nation whose masters still keep millions in concentration camps and who have sworn to bury us.

And the program to loot America to build the Soviet Union is escalating. Remember that the factories we are constructing for the Communists represent the latest in American technology. This technology is unobtainable anywhere else in the world.

Another important thing to remember is the strong possibility that Russian factories using American capital and American technology will, with Soviet slave labor, produce goods which will undersell those produced by American labor in world markets. Just as many thousands of Americans have already lost their jobs to foreign labor (working in European and Asian factories constructed with American foreign aid) still more American workers will see their jobs destroyed by their own government. And these runaway "capitalists" are well aware of the cost benefits of such slave labor.

But as important as jobs are, there is even a more important aspect to the on-going "partnership" between the Rockefellers and the Communists which has been operating for over fifty years. At stake is the very survival of independence and liberty in this country.

Professor Sutton has assembled an abundance of evidence which nobody has even attempted to refute. First, he has shown that Communism is a stagnant system incapable of innovation or high productivity. Its survival, even at a subsistence level for its captives, has required regular transfusions of capital and technology. Without aid from the West, the Soviet Union would have long since collapsed. But without the Soviet Union, the Rockefellers and other super-rich would not have had an "enemy" to justify their schemes for monopoly World Government.

The Soviet Union was first saved by Herbert Hoover with food. Next, came Lenin's New Economic Plan which let the super-capitalists back into Russia. This was followed by FDR's diplomatic recognition of Russia (long advocated by the Rockefellers), which allowed the Soviets to obtain desperately needed credits. World War II turned on the $11 billion Lend-Lease spigot. Following the war, Russia was allowed to denude much of Germany of factories and scientists. During the Kennedy Administration we started providing wheat for hungry Soviet factory workers. During the Vietnam War, America shipped vital supplies to the East European bloc, which was providing North Vietnam with the war equipment to kill our own soldiers. Now we are supplying the world's largest truck factory, extremely sophisticated computers and a cornucopia of other manufacturing technology. To cap the climax, the Wall Street Journal of April 25, 1975, headlines "U.S. Quietly Allows Uranium Shipments to Soviet Union For Processing Into Fuel." Is that unbelievable?

Where was the public outrage that the mediacracy is capable of creating?*

As former Secretary of the Navy James Forrestal observed:

"Consistency never has been a mark of stupidity. If the diplomats who have mishandled our relations with Russia were merely stupid, they would occasionally make a mistake in our favor." In short, what is happening is not just the looting of our economy, but treason. There is something rotten, but it's not in Denmark, it is in Manhattan.

The game plan is simple: We are going to be black-mailed into surrendering or merging with the Soviets. Meanwhile, our Congress wants to stop weapons development so that we can have more welfare programs. Since most of the military budget goes to salaries which cannot be cut, any slashing of "fat" usually means that real muscle—weapons systems—has been amputated.

For five decades the Communists' propaganda line has been that they were going to destroy the Rockefellers and the other super-rich. Yet the Rockefellers have been breastfeeding the Bolshevik monster since its childhood. Today they are leading the parade to provide their Soviet Frankenstein with a high-protein diet. We are supposed to believe those international cartelists do this because they are foolish or greedy. Of course the Rockefellers are greedy for the profits produced by their alliance with the Soviet Union, but that cannot be the total answer. Lenin claimed that capitalists would sell the Communists the

---

*A group of concerned Americans arranged for Sutton, who has testified numerous times before Congressional Committees, to present these facts before the GOP Platform Committee in Miami in 1972. The committee did not show up to hear Sutton's testimony and a scheduled news conference was cancelled. A newsman told Sutton that his story was "too hot" for the newspapers to deal with. When Sutton returned to Hoover, he was ordered by his superiors to make no more public statements during the campaign. Somebody important had obviously made a phone call. Later, Sutton's contract at Hoover was not renewed. He obviously was stepping on too many tender toes.

rope with which they would be hung, if it could be done for a profit. The Rockefellers know that. And now they are building hemp factories in the Soviet Union.

But the Rockefellers are *not* fools. They are brilliant, far-sighted plotters who became immensely powerful by devious Machiavellian planning, and by infiltrating, subsidizing and controlling their opposition.

Plain old-fashioned common sense insists that the Rockefellers know something about Communism that we do not. Since they subsidize it and do not fear it, logic tells us they are either partners with the Communist hierarchy—or they control it.

But if this is true, how do the Rockefellers keep their partners from taking the gun and turning it against their secret backers? We do not pretend to know that answer. There has to be a control mechanism. The Rockefellers would not be so foolish as to let a competitor put a pistol to their heads—let alone provide the pistol. So we must conclude once again that the Rockefellers know something that we do not. Certainly this ultimate secret is known only to the top handful of the conspirators. No researcher is going to learn the answer by pouring over the *New York Times* at his local library.

Because we cannot identify the control mechanism, or describe how it works, many will ridicule our thesis. But, how do they explain the fifty-year Rockefeller program to build the power of Communism? Since the days of John D. Sr., the Rockefellers have prided themselves on their intelligence-gathering capabilities. They know more about their competitor opponents than those competitors know about themselves. You can bet your bippy that the Rockefellers are not naive about the Communists.

But let us assume that they are. Let us assume that in the end the Rockefellers will be the major victims of the Communist empire they have played such an important role in creating. Assume that it has all been done out of sheer stupidity and greed. Where does that put us? Right in the Gulag Archipelago along side them, that's where it puts us.

Either way you lose. The Big Red Machine may or may not devour the Rockefellers. We are convinced it will not, because we believe the Rockefellers and their allies control the comrades who control the guns. But the question is rather academic, because the whole purpose of the Big Red Machine is to swallow *us*! And unless some big changes are made mighty quickly, that's exactly what it will do.

Chapter Ten
The People Planners

It is Kissinger's belief . . . that by controlling food, one can control people, and by controlling energy, especially oil, one can control nations and their financial systems. By placing food and oil under international control along with the world's monetary system, Kissinger is convinced a loosely knit world government can become a reality by 1980.

Paul Scott, Nationally
Syndicated Columnist

The Rockefellers learned nearly a century ago that there are two standard ways for one of their companies to absorb another corporation. If the firm to be acquired is much smaller, a "takeover" is the simplest procedure: buy 'em out. But if the competitor is more your equal, a "merger" must be arranged.

The same principles hold true among nations. No matter how much this country sends abroad as foreign aid, technical assistance, loans that are never repaid, or other largesse, there is simply no way another country—or even a bloc of countries—can be made powerful enough to take us over.

Recognizing this political fact of life, the master planners devised the strategy of a merger—a Great Merger—among nations.

But before such a merger can be consummated, and the United States becomes just another province in a New World Order, there must at least be the semblance of parity among the senior partners in the deal. How does one make the nations of the world more nearly equal? The *Insiders* determined that a two-prong approach was needed; use American money and know-how to build up your competitors, while at the same time use every devious strategy you can devise to weaken and impoverish this country. The goal is not to bankrupt the United States, we must emphasize. Rather, it is to reduce our productive might, and therefore our standard of living, to the meager subsistence level of the socialized nations of the world.

Only a fascist-socialist dictatorship would have the power to accomplish such a "redistribution." Notice that the plan is not to bring the standard of living in less developed countries up to our level, but to bring ours down to meet theirs coming up.

You may be assured, however, that the Rockefellers and their allies are not talking about reducing their *own* quality of life. It is *your* standard of living which must be sacrificed on the altar of the New World Order.

The Rockefeller game plan is to use population, energy, food, and financial controls as a method of *people* control which will lead, steadily and deliberately, into the Great Merger. Much of the spade work for setting up this ploy is being done by Henry Kissinger, who was a personal employee of Nelson Rockefeller for a decade before Rocky placed him in the Nixon Administration. On numerous occasions Herr Kissinger has declared that his goal is to create a "New World Order." Syndicated Washington columnist Paul Scott reveals:

> It is Kissinger's belief, according to his aides, that by controlling food, one can control people, and by controlling energy, especially oil, one can control nations and their financial systems. By placing food and oil under international control along with the world's monetary system, Kissinger is convinced a loosely knit world government operating under the frame-work of the United Nations can become a reality before 1980.

Common sense tells us that a Rockefeller hireling such as Kissinger would not be setting up an "international control" system which takes assets from the Rockefellers and gives them to someone else. Obviously, the game plan is to take other people's assets and put them under the umbrella of a Rockefeller-controlled World Government.

This new strategy may be termed the *crisis* route to World Order. It runs parallel to and eventually will converge with the Atlantic Union *treaty* and *regional government* approach to the Universal State. Washington columnist Paul Scott calls this "the new strategy change from the direct to the indirect approach to bring about world government." The plan, as publicly stated by the CFR's Richard Gardner, part-time State Department functionary and Columbia University Professor of Law and International Organization, amounts to this: Instead of trying to make the UN a complete world dictatorship immediately, the Establishment will identify different problems in different countries. Then they will propose a "solution," which can only be achieved by some kind of international agency, so that each country concerned will be forced to surrender another segment of its national independence. Gardner considers this piecemeal approach the practical road to the end of nationhood:

> We are likely to do better by building our "house of world order" from the bottom up rather than from the top down. It will look like a great "booming, buzzing confusion," to use William James' facetious description of reality; but an end run around national sovereignty, eroding it piece by piece, is likely to get us to world order faster than the old-fashioned frontal assault.

So this is what the Rockefeller gang, working through agents like Kissinger and Gardner, have in mind—an "end run around national sovereignty." Gardner continues, with obvious glee:

> The hopeful aspect of the present situation is that even as nations resist appeals for "world government" and "the surrender of sovereignty," technological, economic and political interests are forcing them to establish more and more far-ranging institutions to manage their mutual interdependence.

One of the most obvious back-door approaches to World Order is through the control of food. The ploy is to establish a World Food Bank, with the necessary goodies supplied (naturally) by the United States. The concept was proposed at the International Monetary Fund Conference in Nairobi by long-time Rockefeller front man Robert S. McNamara (CFR). R. Strange McNamara (yes, that really is his middle name) was made president of the World Bank after he had successfully completed his earlier assignment of crippling this country's military might. McNamara advocated the food-producing nations of the world surrender their surpluses to a "world authority," which would then take charge of redistributing the bounty to the "have-not" nations. The topic was to be discussed at the UN's World Food Conference in Rome in November 1974. Between the time of the original proposal and the Rome conference, Richard Nixon was shuffled into an early retirement and was replaced by a compliant Jerry Ford.

One of Ford's first official acts was to go before the UN General Assembly and assure the international flotsam gathered there that the voice of the Rockefeller's Charlie McCarthy, Henry Kissinger, was the very voice of America in all matters pertaining to international relations. Later, Ford announced that the Secretary of State would appear as keynote speaker on behalf of the United States at the upcoming World Food Conference, superseding the more logical choice, Secretary of Agriculture Earl Butz, who was the official head of the U.S. delegation. Of the hundreds of political commentators around the country, only Paul Scott had the courage to assess the implications of Ford's actions:

> Whether he fully realizes it or not, President Ford has put his stamp of approval on Secretary of State Henry Kissinger's grand design foreign policy for the establishment of a loosely knit world government before the end of the 1970s.
> By calling for the development of a global strategy and policy for food and oil within the structure of the United Nations, the President clearly signaled his acceptance of the "new international order" being sought by Kissinger.

Scott went on to point out that instead of using this nation's enormous food production as a weapon of U.S.

foreign policy, to promote the expansion of freedom throughout the world, Ford accepted Kissinger's plan of passing policy control over U.S. food surpluses, "and eventually all U.S. food," to a national food bank.

Herr Henry made no bones about the fact that all of this is designed to further the New World Order. He told the delegates at Rome: "We are faced not just with the problem of food but with the accelerating momentum of our interdependence." And "our" man in Rome went even further; he declared we should "make global cooperation in food a model for our response to other challenges of an interdependent world — energy, inflation, population, protection of the environment."

Agriculture Secretary Earl Butz admitted of the proposed food bank that "in the end it will be the American taxpayer who pays for it." Who else? And the fact that world-wide distribution of our food will inevitably create food shortages and skyrocketing prices in America has not been overlooked by the Rockefeller conspirators. That is part of the plan.

And before you conclude that any such program would be emphatically rejected by an angry American electorate, remember this: by the time the plan is implemented, the UN will have an army to back up its looting of America! Doubtless the clan's minions in the bureaucracy and the media will refer to the planned food shortage as a "mandatory national diet program."*

The whole thrust of the Rome gathering was that it is the obligation of the United States—which means you, the worker and taxpayer—to feed the world. This, despite the fact that for years America has supplied more than 80

---

*While U.S. reserves of food and feed grains are already being depleted, Russia and Communist China have quietly been using part of their massive purchases of bargain-priced American grain to build up their stockpiles. Crews of U.S. and foreign ships carrying U.S. grain to Russian and Chinese ports have been told by Communist dock workers that every third or fourth shipment of U.S. grain is being placed in permanent storage facilities as part of those countries' national reserves.

percent of the food given to foreign countries. It is such American giveaways that in recent years have provided over $25 billion in foodstuffs to such ingrates as Marxist India, now a dictatorship openly allied with the Soviet Union, where the bulk of our grains winds up feeding rats, not hungry people.

At least $200 billion in such aid has been similarly squandered to more than 125 nations—including more millions now going to members of the OPEC cartel, which has quadrupled oil prices. To pay for all of these give-aways, the *Insiders* who run the show have used printing press inflation money to add hundreds of billions of dollars to our National Debt. This, coupled with the consequent reduction of domestic supplies, has sent our own food prices out of sight.

But, at least in the past our stupidity was of our own doing and under our own control. Informed Americans could have stopped it—and could still stop it today—by throwing the Congressmen who voted for the giveaways out of office. In the future, when the Rockefeller-Kissinger plan for the international authority over food is implemented, our food supply will no longer be under our control. What then?

Increasingly we hear plaintive bleats from the Rocke-fellers' sheep in the media, calling for Americans to make increased sacrifices to feed the rest of the world. Incredible as it may seem, the truth-twisters of the airwaves and press are attempting to make us feel guilty that we are not starving.

None of these Rockefeller lackeys dares suggest, of course, that the difference between American agricultural production and the poverty levels of the so-called "have-not" nations is the difference between individualism, with its reliance on private property and free enterprise, and feudalism-fascism-socialism-collectivism. It is the difference between incentives and a planned economy; between efficiency and wasteful boondoggles; between a million salesmen pushing the "too much" and a million ration clerks dividing up the "too little."

This is not to say America's agricultural system is perfect. To the extent that we have instituted price supports and subsidies, paying men not to grow food, we have suffered. Nevertheless, the success of American agriculture under freedom is a model the rest of the world should be encouraged to copy.

But if more nations achieved independence in food production, much of the impetus for world government would disappear faster than a freeloader when the check arrives. In order for the Rockefellers to achieve their New World Order, first they must create famines and the fear of further suffering. All that is required to create a famine is to put all agriculture under control of government bureaucracy, then wait awhile. The bigger the bureaucracy the shorter the wait, and international bureaucracy is the *ne plus ultra* in producing red tape instead of wheat.

Intertwined with food production grab is the push for population control. People planning is an important tool in building the net that will drag us fishes into the New World Order. The "population bomb," real or exaggerated, is being used in conjunction with food, energy, and international money problems as part of the One-Big-Brother snare.

Coinciding with the UN-sponsored conferences in Nairobi and Rome, the United Nations sponsored the World Population Conference at Bucharest, Romania in August 1974. Headlining the program was none other than John D. Rockefeller III, who proclaimed: "I come to Bucharest with an urgent call for a deep and probing reappraisal of all that has been done in the population field. I have changed my mind and now believe family planning alone is not adequate."

An Associated Press report explained: "Rockefeller . . . has for years been one of the world's leading advocates of family planning. He donated millions of dollars toward population research and is founder and chairman of the Population Council, a private U.S. organization funded largely by [millions of dollars] the Rockefeller and Ford Foundations." The wire service continued: "His speech reflected the viewpoint voiced at this conference by many members of the Third World and Socialist [that is, Communist] countries." John D. III obviously felt right at home behind the Iron Curtain, as he called for a redistribution of wealth and piously proclaimed that modern development should emphasize "an equitable distribution of the fruits of progress."

In his remarks to the gathering of people planners, the eldest of the Royal Rockefellers made three main points: First, he echoed the Communist line that the rich must give their wealth to the poor. Second, he asserted that voluntary family planning is inadequate and called for Big Brother to start dictating whether or not a couple is permitted to have a baby. Third, in calling for "moderate levels of consumption" in advanced nations, Rockefeller advocated that Americans voluntarily reduce their standard of living.

The fact that it is a little incongruous—not to say hypocritical—for a man whose family is worth uncounted millions, who has thousands of servants, hundreds of luxurious homes and lives in an opulence unknown by the oriental potentates of yore, to ask the rest of his fellow citizens to scale down their living standards, went unnoticed in the *New York Times*. But to belabor the obvious, whose wealth do you think Rockefeller wants to share, yours or his?

Going along with the call by Rockefeller (who claimed the "United Nations is the world's highest authority" for governmental control over people), the conference set in motion the machinery to institutionalize the totalitarian demands of the Stop the Storkers.

The *Washington Post*, a chief Establishment mouthpiece, has discussed the Nazilike policies being advocated by the people planners:

> The day may be approaching when couples will have to prove eligibility and demonstrate qualifications before they are permitted to become parents.
> Or there may be baby ration cards for couples, group marriages, mass distribution of antifertility drugs, parent

licensing, legal polygamy, abortions on demand, more varied life options for women and more restricted ones for men—such as forced paternity leave for new fathers.

Understand that such enforced infertility is not planned for India or Senegal, but for the United States, where zero population growth is already a fact.

All this, despite the provable fact that there is ample room on earth for all of us—in fact, if every man, woman and child in the entire world moved to the State of Washington, (twentieth in size of all the states), each would have 490 square feet of space.

But we are being led to believe that unless we give Big Brother total power over people's rights to have children, we will all be ankle deep in human beings within a decade. Such august organizations as the National Academy of Sciences are helping to hawk this Rockefeller line, with doomsday messages such as: "There can be no doubt concerning the long-term prognosis. Either the birth rate of the world must come down or the death rate must go back up."

This is not to discount the possibility that overpopulation, particularly in backward nations, cannot be a genuine problem. But, if the Rockefellers were truly interested in curbing population growth *without* enslaving everybody, there is a much better solution. When a country's standard of living goes up, the birth rate goes down—voluntarily. Assist nations such as India and Red China to benefit by the adoption of free market, private property principles, and the abundance produced by such newly free peoples would astound the world. The Rockefellers, however, are interested in more controls, not fewer problems.

The specious Rockefeller argument that the world must accept Mao-style people control or perish is so phony that it is amazing the conspirators have gotten anyone to buy it. As Reverend R. J. Rushdoony points out in his excellent book, *The Myth of Overpopulation*:

Socialism always creates ultimately an imbalance between the number of people living and their food supply which results in hunger or famine. There is in this sense therefore always a problem of overpopulation under socialism. Socialism, moreover, affects both the food supply, by limiting it, and also the population, by both expanding it at one stage and limiting it at another.

To the Rockefellers, socialism is not a system for redistributing wealth—especially not for redistributing their wealth—but a system to control people and competitors. Socialism puts power in the hands of the government. And since the Rockefellers control the government, government control means Rockefeller control. You may not have known this, but you can be sure they do!

When the Rockefellers join the UN's World Population Conference in calling for the promotion "of a new economic order by eradicating the cause of world poverty, by ensuring the equitable distribution of the world resources, by eliminating the injustices of existing world trade systems and exploitation perpetrated by capitalistic . . . corporations," something smells as fishy as an unwashed tuna boat.

Curbing population growth is just part of the Rockefeller war on the American family. Abortion is another. According to John H. Knowles, president of the Rockefeller Foundation and one of America's foremost promoters of the slaughter of the unborn, the goal of the Foundation is to achieve the capacity in America for 1.8 million abortions every year.

Not coincidentally, it was John D. Rockefeller III who was appointed by Richard Nixon as chairman of the newly created Commission on Population Growth and the American Future. In accepting the appointment, John D. III pontificated:

The average citizen doesn't appreciate the social and economic implications of population growth and what it does to the quality of all our lives. Rather than think of population control as a negative thing, we should see that it can be enriching.

One of the early reports of the Rockefeller Commission recommended:

> ... that present state laws restricting abortion be liberalized along the lines of the New York State Statute, such abortions to be performed on request by duly licensed physicians under conditions of medical safety.

And the Commisssion further suggested that "federal, state, and local governments make funds available to support abortion services in states with liberalized statutes." Rockefeller is so callous about individual beliefs that he would forcibly extract money from Catholic taxpayers, among others, to finance what their religion teaches is the murder of the unborn. Tough rocks, says the Rock: "Religious preconceptions must be overcome."

The New York model abortion law which chairman John enthusiastically applauded was passed, of course, under the leadership of brother Nelson. During the Vice Presidential confirmation hearings Dr. Charles Rice, Professor of Law at the Notre Dame Law School, characterized Nelson as "the incarnate symbol of the anti-life movement," and said that Mr. Rockefeller "is perhaps the leading proponent of permissive abortion in the United States."

The Rockefellers have even financed the establishment of an abortion mill. In the summer of 1971, Planned Parenthood-New York City opened its first large scale abortion center—a prototype for the development of additional centers throughout the city, state, and nation. The center was originally designed to perform more than 10,-000 abortions a year for an average fee of $80, with funds provided in many cases by Medicaid. The initial funds to establish the abortion mill came from a $200,000 pledge from The Rockefeller Brothers Fund.

The past three generations of Rockefellers have not been notoriously considerate of other people's feelings and beliefs. When a group of pro-life activists picketed a speech by Nelson Rockefeller in Nebraska, the loveable old politician told a 15-year old girl: "Don't knock it [abortion], girl, you might need one someday."

In all wars this nation has fought, from the battle of Lexington in 1776 through the last fatality in Vietnam, American combat deaths totaled 668,226 men. Yet, in just the single year of 1972, 700,000 innocent babes were killed in this country, legally, before they could draw their first breath. (Current estimates are that this figure could increase to 1.6 million abortions a year.) That is the price of the Rockefellers' promotion of easy abortion in the United States. But it is just part of the price all of us will pay (and pay, and pay), if the people planners succeed in herding all of us into their New World Order.

Yes, the Rockefellers are planners. As John D.'s aide, Fred Gates, once confessed: "In our dreams we have limitless resources and the people yield themselves with perfect docility to our moulding hands." Now, thanks to the taxpayers, the Rockefellers have almost limitless funds. As a result, faceless bureaucrats in Washington—whom you did not hire and whom you cannot fire—now tell you how to run your business, whom you may hire, where your children will be bussed to school, what products you can purchase, and even what foods you can and cannot eat. It is only a matter of time until the dicto-crats tell you how many children you are permitted to have.

There is nothing wrong with planning. The question is who is doing it. Our Founding Fathers believed people should be free to plan their own lives. The Rockefellers believe their agents in the federal government must plan your life for you. It is a simple choice: Will you run your own life, or will you be forced to obey the dictates of bureaucrats, social workers, college professors, sociolo-gists, psychologists, and others who are fronting for the House of Rockefeller?

Nelson is very candid about it. In an October 1975 in-terview in *Playboy* magazine, Rocky admitted: "I'm a great believer in planning. Economic, social, political, military, *total world planning*." (Emphasis added.)

When Big Brother arrives, he may well be wearing horn-rimmed glasses.

Chapter Eleven
The Great Energy Swindle

The craziest notion that has hit this country in a long while . . . is that shortages of gas, beef and a lot of other things are bad for the American people. What America needs is more shortages.

James Reston (CFR),
New York Times

Having set the wheels in motion for establishing international controls over food and population, the Rockefellers then made their move in the all-important energy field. As Dr. Medford Evans has noted: "Energy makes the world go 'round." And he adds the obvious, but crucial fact: "Who controls what makes the world go 'round controls the world." In other words, when the New World Order controls the planet's energy, the world dictatorship will be established.

Syndicated columnist Paul Scott informs us: "Once [the] concept of international policy control over food is accepted by UN members, Kissinger then plans to move to establish this same concept over oil and eventually all energy in the world."

You will recall that in the last chapter we quoted a report by Mr. Scott that Kissinger believes that by controlling energy, especially oil, the *Insiders* can control nations and their financial systems; and that such international controls of oil and monetary systems could bring about a world government *within the next five years*.

But according to the Rockefeller-Kissinger game plan, before oil can be internationalized, there must be a crisis which threatens to bring about a worldwide depression. Remember, "crises . . . are the great federators." There can be little doubt that the current international petroleum crisis has been deliberately contrived. It was engineered from start to finish. The planning involves typical bureaucratic idiocy which may or may not have been intended to have the result which it inevitably did; and to conspiratorial planning by Rockefeller agents who at all times knew exactly what they were doing.

Contrary to the incantations of the doomsayers, America is *not* running out of oil. As Don Oakley of the Copley News Service notes: "For every one of the billions upon billions of barrels of petroleum the United States has consumed since Colonel Drake drilled the first well in 1859, at least another barrel remains in the ground." According to John Knight, editorial chairman of the Knight newspapers: "A figure of 100 billion barrels [of oil reserves] is offered as conservative, although some studies place the figure at several hundred billion barrels excluding shale oil."

Get that? We are sitting on several hundred billion barrels *excluding* shale. Yet even today the United States consumes only about six billion barrels of oil a year.

Shale oil is oil locked up in porous rock. The Interior Department estimates our "easily" recoverable shale oil at eighty billion barrels, and shale oil recoverable with intensive technology at six hundred billion barrels. The six hundred billion barrels that appear to be recoverable are enough to last one hundred years at the present rate of consumption. However, most U.S. shale resources are on federal lands in Wyoming, Colorado, and Utah. None is yet being produced commercially because the federal government has been very slow—some say suspiciously slow—to permit development of this crucial resource.

We are literally surrounded by oil. *U.S. News & World Report* stated as far back as November 22, 1971 that our total offshore oil reserves amount to approximately 780 billion barrels. This does not, of course, include the estimated twenty billion barrels of oil in Alaska. Counting only the offshore oil, the Alaskan reserves and the easily recovered shale oil, the United States has 880 *billion* barrels of oil reserves. At the current rate of consumption, my calculator says that this is enough oil to last beyond the year 2121. That is a lot longer than any of us is going to last. Surely we can produce alternative forms of power and energy in that amount of time!

Why is it, asks economist Tom Rose, that after over three hundred years of continuous material progress in America, without fuel shortages, we should suddenly stumble upon an energy crisis in 1973? If America has abundant fuel supplies, why aren't they abundantly available? Could it be, asks Professor Rose, that the historical process by which these supplies have been made available has changed? He observes:

> Historically, energy in America has been supplied by profit-seeking private entrepreneurs and profit-oriented corporations. These risk-takers have invested millions and millions of dollars every year in their long-range plans to supply the ever-growing energy needs of the American people. Historically, they have adjusted their production plans to price signals received through the competitive marketplace. For over three centuries this free market process has been eminently successful. And competing sources of energy have always been in abundant supply at reasonable prices.

In recent decades, however, the bureaucrats and the politicians have thrust themselves into the market process. As Professor Rose notes, "during the last two or three decades—especially since 1955 when the FPC (Federal Power Commission) started controlling the wellhead price of gas and oil—energy suppliers have faced non-market signals . . . Neither the Mideast war nor American prosperity has caused our present energy crisis. It was caused by political meddling."

That last point is so crucial to understanding the mess we are in that we want to repeat it. Fuelish, oil-consuming Americans didn't cause the energy crisis. The Mideast war didn't cause it. Our growing prosperity didn't cause it. Political meddling (by some of the brightest "planners" around, we might add) did.

Have you heard the Rockefellers, Standard Oil execs, or

even other petroleum countries screaming bloody murder about the fact that a bunch of paper-shuffling bureaucrats have so distorted the realities of supply and demand that we now face a worldwide crisis? Yes, Mobil has run a few ads hinting at this. But, if the Rockefellers really wanted to demonstrate what a palpable fraud the energy crisis really is, they would be showing 60-minute documentary specials on ABC, NBC and CBS. Instead, these networks have produced a spate of specials to bamboozle the public into believing we are down to our last gallon of Exxon.

One of the major excuses for the massive interference by government in the development and marketing of energy resources has been the ecology movement. The "crisis" used to strangle development of offshore oil began with the Santa Barbara oil spill in 1969. The "Liberal" media heralded the Santa Barbara spill as a greater disaster than the bubonic plague. Television newswatchers were treated every night to heart-rending closeups of gooey gulls covered with crude oil.

A study of the Santa Barbara spill was subsequently undertaken by forty leading scientists under the direction of Dr. Dale Straughan, a marine biologist from the University of Southern California. This $250,000 study produced a 900-page report which declared: "Not only had overall damage by the spill been greatly overestimated, but where damage had been done, nature had returned it to normal."

The conclusions of Dr. Straughan and her team became one of the biggest secrets since the whereabouts of Judge Crater. The Brinkleys, Cronkites, and others who had made a national horror story of the unfortunate spill were so busy beating the drums to stop all offshore drilling that they didn't have time to cover the less dramatic, truthful story of what really happened in Santa Barbara. They were too preoccupied with promoting a shortage-producing power grab by government to report that out of approximately fourteen thousand offshore wells which have been drilled, there have been a grand total of three—yes, *three*—serious oil spills.

The phony propaganda about the Santa Barbara spill was the excuse used by the Nixon Administration to cancel leases and strangle offshore oil and gas drilling, not only in Santa Barbara Channel, but around the nation. Just as it had done time and time again, the Administration surrendered to the cries of the mob and kept silent about the known facts. While consumption of petroleum and gas was jumping every year, the Nixon poohbahs put the lid on expansion of supply. Anybody who has plodded his way through elementary economics knows that if demand increases while supplies and prices remain the same, the inevitable result will be a shortage. The masters of Nixonomics knew what they were doing, and they did it anyway.

But stopping further offshore drilling was not the only plus from the Santa Barbara oil spill for the creators of our shortages. In the wake of this "ecological disaster," Senator Henry Jackson of Washington was able to put through his oft-defeated bill to establish a national policy on environmental protection and to create the Council on Environmental Quality. The law seemed innocent enough at first glance. But, as Dan Smoot relates in *The Business End of Government*:

> . . . it was a sleeper, as activist attorneys exultantly called it after it was safely on the statute books. This legislation provided the activists with legal standing to make court attacks against major business activities throughout the United States . . . .
>
> The environmental-policy law left the definition of environment so vague and open-ended that it gave federal courts almost limitless power to veto the actions of Executive agencies and the laws of Congress. No business can initiate a major activity without first dealing with a government agency of some kind—about permits, licenses, rights-of-way leases, land leases, use of public thoroughfares, and so on. Any group of two or more people willing to post a small bond and engage an attorney can bring court action against a government agency, alleging that, in granting permission for a business activity, the agency failed to file an adequate environmental-impact

statement as required by the National Environmental Policy Act of 1969. They can demand a court injunction to halt the business activity until the government agency files an adequate impact statement and suggests an alternative approach.

The Jackson Bill, which Richard Nixon refused to veto, was used to delay the construction of the Alaskan pipeline for an incredible five years. Under the guise of keeping the tundra virginal for the dainty hooves of caribou, the ecomaniacs tied up the pipeline project in the courts. A pipeline across the frozen tundra of central Alaska is about as conspicuous as a thread stretching from the eighth to the ninth hole of a golf course—and about as harmful to the game. But the Jackson Environment Law gave the radicals not only respectability in the courts, but a legal club that declared any developers must be assumed *guilty* until they proved their innocence.

Stung by public outrage, Congress finally acted to allow the contractors to begin construction of the pipeline. So after a five-year delay, we can look forward to crude pouring out the end of that pipeline sometime in 1978. But had the Nixon Administration not gone smilingly down to defeat at the hands of the ecomaniacs, Alaskan crude would now be flowing into refineries at the rate of one million barrels a day—which just happens to be almost the same amount that the U.S. has been importing from the Middle East. Needless to say, the Sierra Clubbers are about as popular in Alaska as Bobby Riggs at a baby shower for Gloria Steinem.

One of the most important moves in the effort to create artificial shortages of petroleum occurred in June 1970, when President Nixon issued an Executive Order creating the Environmental Protection Agency. A preliminary Report on the activities of the 9,000 bureaucrats in the EPA has now been issued by the House Appropriation Subcommittee. It declares:

The subcommittee is convinced that the Environmental Protection Agency has played a major role in the current energy crisis. The approval by the agency of overly restrictive state plans, which call for the meeting of primary and secondary ambient air standards at the same time, has resulted in the need for the industry to convert from coal to low sulfur fuels. This increased requirement for oil and gas has been a major contributor to our current fuel problems.

In addition, the automobile emission control standards imposed by the agency have greatly increased the requirements for gasoline, which is also in short supply and will probably require rationing.

Mr. Nixon's Environmental Protection Agency, in the name of controlling air pollution, has forced auto manufacturers to pile all kinds of gas-eating gadgets onto our motors. The net result has been a drop of at least twenty percent in mileage, and considering the near impossibility of keeping such engines properly tuned, the loss may be as high as fifty percent.

According to Shirley Scheibla, *Barron's* Washington editor, the gadgets applied to our cars by the EPA now result in the use of 300,000 extra barrels of gasoline a day; by 1980, the controls will require the consumption of an added two million gallons of gasoline a day. Meanwhile, federally required reduction of lead in gasoline has reduced fuel efficiency by another twenty percent. And, no two experts even seem to agree on whether the required gadgetry actually decreases pollution. Some think that the net effect is an increase. We don't pretend to know, but it seems to us that if our car is burning up to twice as much gasoline, the net amount of pollutants coming out the exhaust pipe has probably increased.

The ten thousand independent oil companies in the U.S. drill 80 percent of the wells. Government or "people" control of the oil industry would, in practice, mean Rockefeller control over their competitors. It would mean the death knell for the independents and create One Big Oil Company under the sway of the House of Rockefeller. Yes, competition is still a sin.

If you still have any lingering doubts about the Rockefellers promoting the energy shortage for power and profit, consider the fact they have financed their alleged enemies, the ecomaniacs.

Incredible, you say? Well, it's true. And for reasons other than the Rockefellers' love of blue sky and falling profits. The "environmental legislation" pushed through Congress was based on lobbying by innumerable "experts." Putting together these "citizens lobbies" takes *lots* of money; and contrary to the hokey publicity from most such groups, the dollars do not come from school children donating their milk money—or even from college students foregoing a beer. The money to fight "the entrenched interests" comes largely from those same entrenched interests, and the foundations which they have created. It represents the old ploy of Bre'r Rabbit begging Bre'r Bear not to throw him into the briar patch. Only in this case, Bre'r Rabbit is the Rockefellers and the briar patch is socialistic controls. Remember, more controls mean worse shortages; and when oil and gas are scarce, prices go right through the skylight.*

During Congressional Hearings on the National Environmental Policy Act of 1969, none other than J. G. Harrar, then president of the Rockefeller Foundation (and a CFR member, of course), advocated the United Nations developing an international program for dealing with worldwide pollution. Other lobbyists who joined the clamor for more government controls were financed by the Ford Foundation, which is more closely interlocked with the Rockefellers than two teenagers in the last row of a drive-in movie. Edward Rogers, general counsel of the Ford-backed Environmental Defense Fund, actually advocated *international* control of automobiles.

The testimony at such hearings and the lists of those presenting it are monotonously repetitious. In one way or another all those appearing favored an increase in federal control over the "environment"—which boils down to

---

*About one-third of the cost of a gallon of gas goes to the oil company. When gasoline reaches one dollar a gallon, as most experts anticipate, Standard Oil's share will be a lot bigger than when you could fillerup at 34.9¢

federal controls over almost everything and everybody. Some witnesses, less sophisticated than their mentors, boldly called for the destruction of the capitalist system; others suggested that "regional" or "international" planning agencies are needed to cope with pollution.

The loud-mouth Marxists have relatively little impact on Congress, of course. It is the corporate socialists in the Brooks Brothers suits who are really dangerous. They bring with them the credibility, prestige and financial backing of the Rockefeller complex, and you can be sure Congress listens to them *very* closely.

Although it seems to have been around forever, the environmental movement appeared on the national scene almost overnight. Five years ago, not one person in a thousand had even heard the word *ecology*. But suddenly all of us were supposed to panic at the thought of the slimy hand of pollution suffocating us as we sleep.

The major bankrollers of this "spontaneous" movement were the numerous Rockefeller foundations, the Rockefeller-controlled Ford Foundation, the Rockefeller-controlled Carnegie Foundation and the Rockefeller-interlocked Mellon (Gulf Oil) foundations. Among the most vigorous public advocates were Robert O. Anderson of Atlantic Richfield (and the CFR) and Henry Ford II of the Ford Motor Company (and the CFR).

The number one piggy bank for the "ecology" movement has been the Ford Foundation, almost all of whose trustees are members of the Rockefellers' CFR. It has poured millions of dollars into hustling population planning and environmental controls of every sort.

The Ford Foundation gave $2 million to the Energy Policy Project to aid it in the creation of a federal energy policy. For that sum of money, it expected results, and it got them. Ford also gave $309,000 to the Center for Law in the Public Interest and $162,000 to the Royal Institute of International Affairs (the English counterpart of our CFR) to study the role of oil companies in the energy market!

The most effective organization in using law suits to force Zero Economic Growth on the country—by blocking construction of refineries, airports, shopping centers, housing and every other form of development—is the Sierra Club. The Sierra Club was for many years a respected group honestly promoting conservation and preservation of forests and wildlife, until it was taken over by political radicals. Now, using the Environmental Protection Act, it has used the courts to throw hundreds of thousands of workers out of jobs.

The Sierra Club is the very symbol of the ecology movement's fight against the "big corporations". Supplying the funds for its allegedly humanitarian crusade is—you guessed it!—the Ford Foundation. Ford made grants to the Sierra Club Legal Defense Fund of $98,000 in 1971 and $143,000 in 1972, and the Rockefellers have also donated to the Sierra Club Legal Defense Fund.

Next to the Ford Foundation, the leading funders of the ecology movement are the various Rockefeller foundations. The Rockefeller Brothers Fund, the Rockefeller Foundation and the Rockefeller Family Fund are all contributing heavily to the environmental revolution from which Standard Oil is profiting so handsomely by driving petroleum prices into orbit.

We realize that this sounds like something out of Ripley's "Believe It or Not." But here are the facts:

In 1969, the Rockefeller Foundation donated $250,000 to the Academy of National Sciences; $200,000 to the American Conservation Association; $60,000 to the National Audubon Society; and, $25,000 to the Conservation Fund.

In 1970, the Rockefeller Brothers Fund gave $500,000 to the Population Council. The Rockefeller Foundation gave ecology grants of $10,000 to the New School for Social Research, and $10,000 to the Population Reference Bureau.

In 1971, the Rockefeller Foundation gave $300,000 to Citizens for a Quieter City; $23,200 to Columbia University Center for Policy Research; $500,000 to the Conservation Foundation; $152,000 to the Environmental Law Institute; $50,000 in ecology funds to the Massachusetts

Institute of Technology; and, $1,000,000 to the Population Council.

In 1972, the Rockefeller Family Fund gave $10,000 to the National Resources Defense Council; and two grants, one for $17,750 and one for $25,000, to the Sierra Club Legal Defense Fund. The Rockefeller Foundation donated $25,000 to M.I.T. for environmental studies, and the Rockefeller Brothers Fund donated $500,000 to the American Conservation Association.

And, in 1973, the Rockefeller Foundation gave $500,000 to the Population Council and $25,000 to the Population Crisis Committee. The Rockefeller Brothers Fund donated $250,000 to the Population Council, $10,000 to the Population Council, and $25,000 to the Population Institute.

It should be mentioned that it is illegal for foundations to finance political activities. If the law were enforced, these foundations would lose their tax exemption. But don't hold your breath until this happens. The IRS's sauce for your goose is not sauce for the Rockefellers' gander.

Typical of the bilge pumped out by the organizations bankrolled by the Rockefellers is this *Los Angeles Times* report of August 27,1975:

> Americans will have to eat less, switch from cars to bicycles and adopt other belt-tightening measures in the next decade because the energy shortage is here to stay, according to a paper published by the Aspen Institute for Humanistic Studies. The paper's author, Abraham M. Sirkin, a former member of the State Department's policy and planning staff, predicts the cutbacks will produce a generation of healthier Americans.

The Aspen Institute, we hope you will *not* be surprised to learn, is funded by the Rockefeller Brothers Fund.

The Rockefellers are not the only oil interests helping to finance the ostensibly anti-oil ecology movement. Major donors have been Gulf Oil Foundation, the Humble Companies Charitable Trust, the Mobil Foundation and the Union Oil of California Foundation. All, of course, are either Rockefeller-controlled or interlocked with the

Rockefellers through the CFR. These groups in essence paid for the legislation which has killed the mileage obtained by automobiles. But, the ultimate stakes are much bigger—using the continued energy crisis as the rationale for the creation of the New World Order.

Ralph Nader, the man who once told an audience that what we need is "some kind of communism," is also bankrolled by the Rockefeller network in his attempt to destroy the free enterprise system. Among the groups financing the Caped Crusader are the ubiquitous Ford Foundation and the Field Foundation, both CFR interlocked. Nader is not really fighting the Establishment. He works for it. According to a *Business Week* article reprinted in the *Congressional Record* of March 10, 1971, John D. Rockefeller IV is even an advisor to Nader.

Naturally, the shortages of petroleum which have been artificially created in the U.S. has made us dependent on foreign oil. In order to calm an angry public, there has been much talk of taking off the political restrictions and achieving "energy independence." It is strictly a smokescreen. While talking independence, the Rockefeller conspirators are planning to keep us dependent on foreign oil. After all, they own or market most of that foreign oil.

In the *Wall Street Journal* for March 6, 1974, Henry Kissinger admitted the talk about "energy independence" was a fraud. Project Independence is merely "a way station on the road to a new Project Interdependence." And at the World Energy Conference in Detroit during September 1974, President Ford, speaking without any detectable ventriloquist's strings, declared: "I call on all of you to respond to the challenge and to propose to the world your recommendations for a global energy strategy. Whether you call it Project Interdependence, or some other name, is not the essential point." It is the "interdependence" which is essential. The created crises in energy, food, and population are straw men, set up by the *Insiders* so they can be knocked down—and a "New World Order" can be established. Yes, crises are the great federator.

Kissinger's plan to maneuver international policy control over oil is beginning to emerge, and, as Paul Scott notes, it "is one of the most intriguing stories of our times."

According to Paul Scott, officials at the World Bank have estimated that the flow of Western dollars to oil producers in the Middle East is "now running at the rate of $100 billion a year—or more than all of U.S. investments abroad. To put it in the most stark terms, the Middle East oil producers are accumulating so much wealth from the Western industrial nations that they will be able—if current prices continue—to buy them out by 1980."

With OPEC gaining control of most of the world's oil and money, Kissinger sees a confrontation situation developing between oil producers and consumers, reports Scott, out of which will arise "the internationalization of oil production, pricing and distribution." It would be the ultimate monopoly.

Very conceivably the Arab sheiks are being set up to trigger a war in the Middle East. Remember, Kissinger is already on record as stating that we might invade the Middle East if oil is embargoed. With the super-sophisticated military equipment we are providing the sheiks the war would be a bloody one—especially if it, like the arranged wars in Vietnam and Korea before it, is fought under the UN banner. The end result, of course, would be the "internationalization of oil."

Again, only the naive will think that the Rockefellers are having their agent Kissinger arrange the "internationalization of oil" so that the Oilbucks can be stripped of their holdings. The prospects of such a scenario should make any independent oil developer in the world worry. Competition is still a sin, and monopoly is still the name of the Rockefeller game.

While Armegeddon is being set up in the Middle East, the Rockefellers are preparing to stick John Q. Taxpayer with the bill for the world's oil deficits. A story in the *Chicago Tribune* of October 2, 1974, is headlined "U.S.

To Back New Way to Foot World Oil Bills—Simon."
Secretary of the Treasury William Simon, an international
banker and CFR member, told leaders of the World Bank
and International Monetary Fund that if "developing
nations" were having difficulty paying the oil tab, they
need look no farther than the American taxpayer. "If there
is a clear need for additional international lending
mechanisms, the United States will support their
establishment," he said.

Under the Kissinger-Rockefeller plan, Americans will
pay the bills in more ways than one. Without a peep of
complaint from the kept press, Kissinger met with
members of the International Energy Agency and agreed
to share our oil with them in case the Rockefellers stage
another Arab oil boycott. Unkept columnist Paul Scott
reveals:

> Under the oil-sharing plan worked out recently in
> Brussels by the U.S. and 11 other major industrial
> countries, for example, domestically produced oil in the
> U.S. for the first time in our history would be shared and
> allocated in case of another Middle East oil embargo.
>
> Precise allocations would be worked out by a quasi-
> independent management organization set up within the
> Paris-based Organization for Economic Cooperation and
> Development, an economic consultive grouping of
> leading non-Communist industrial nations.
>
> Most puzzling and alarming part of this Kissinger oil
> plan is that it in effect puts the "triggering device" in the
> hands of the Middle East oil producers—thus increasing
> the power of their oil weapon and making it more tempting
> for the Arabs to use.
>
> For control over U.S. domestic oil to pass into the hands
> of an international body, all the Middle East oil producers
> now need do is impose their oil embargo as they did during
> the 1973 Arab-Israeli war.

The control over agriculture and energy as part of the
Rockefeller-Kissinger strategy for looting the country
is the core of the *Insiders'* plan to force Zero Economic
Growth on the country.

Leading the call for ZEG is a group of international

establishmentarians called The Club of Rome. The Club is described by author Ovid Demaris in *Dirty Business* as "an organization of distinguished industrialists, bankers and scientists from twenty-five countries." The Club was created at the Rockefeller family's private estate at Bellagio, Italy. The Club put out a report which warned that, unless the standard of living of the developed nations was severly restricted, "A rather sudden and uncontrollable decline in both population and industrial capacity" was inevitable.

Here we have fifty key businessmen and international bankers gathering under the auspices of the Rockefeller family and coming to the conclusion that production in America should be reduced! Again, understand that it is your standard of living they are proposing to decimate, not their own.

Naturally, the controlled press did everything possible to legitimize the scare stories concocted by the Roman clubbers. For example, here is how *Time* magazine portrayed their predictions in a feature story on January 24, 1972:

> The furnaces of Pittsburgh are cold; the assembly lines of Detroit are still. In Los Angeles, a few gaunt survivors of a plague desperately till freeway center strips, backyards and outlying fields, hoping to raise a subsistence crop. London's offices are dark, its docks deserted. In the farm lands of the Ukraine, abandoned tractors litter the fields; there is no fuel for them. The waters of the Rhine, Nile and Yellow rivers reek with pollutants.

The message from these fright peddlers appeared in a 197-page paperback which was published in eighteen editions and made available in twenty-three languages, including Serbo-Croation, Finnish, and Thai. The *Insiders* who run the show know that the only way to achieve surrender by consent is to frighten Americans into supinely accepting their plans.

Before continuing, however, we feel duty bound to assure you that, despite the huzzahs from the chorus of the CFR-controlled media, the Rockefeller-sponsored "study," titled *The Limits To Growth*, was (and is) considered absurd by informed demographers. Wilfred Beckerman, the respected professor of political economy at the University of London, went so far as to call the book "a brazen piece of impudence." (Which is the harshest language you will ever hear a proper Englishman use.)

Our only hope for survival, the ecological fright peddlers assure us, is ZPG combined with ZEG. America has already reached Zero Population Growth, but putting enough brakes on our economy to achieve Zero Economic Growth has been a hayburner of a different hue. Only direct government intervention can assure ZEG as advocated by the Club of Rome.

Clickety-clack, clickety-clack, the message is being dutifully parroted by the Establishment media as its propaganda machines grind out the doctrine of survival through a lowered standard of living. Features like "Running Out of Everything" (*Newsweek*) and "Time For A New Frugality" (*Time*) have been appearing with regularity in the slick weeklies. Much of the propaganda has been geared towards making Americans feel guilt for their prosperity and shame for their alleged greed and profligacy.

So what is the solution? There is only one way to stop the profit system and that is by direct government intervention (which can take a wide variety of forms—taxation, regulation, allocation, rationing, etc.). The two words most often used to describe such governmental actions are of course, socialism and fascism.

But, proponents of socialism within the Establishment are careful never, ever, to use the word. While outspoken radicals are less hypocritical, Liberal politicians, bureaucrats, and media managers are aware that mainstream Americans know what socialism means, and they want no part of it. So the Establishment salesmen for socialism, who for thirty years have been implementing it while the radicals talk about it, always use code words and euphemisms. Instead of calling socialism or fascism by their right names, the Establishment prefers terms like planning. The question is: Who is going to plan your life, you or the Frankenstein monster created by the Rockefellers, called Big Brother?

If the Rockefeller-CFR clique has an official spokesman, it is James Reston, leading columnist of the *New York Times* whose syndicated column appears in hundreds of papers across the nation. Read Reston and you can keep up with the latest Rockefeller-Establishment *line*. In 1973, Reston wrote:

> The craziest notion that has hit this country in a long while—and we've had quite a few nutty notions lately—is that shortages of gas, beef and a lot of other things are bad for the American people.
>
> What America really needs is more shortages. It is not our shortages but our surpluses that are hurting us. Too much gas, too much booze, and—fire me tomorrow!—too much newsprint are our problem. . . .

Yes, you read that correctly. James Reston of the *New York Times* says that what we need are more shortages. Like playing for a losing football team, shortages build character. The more we are deprived, the better off we will be! Of course, the worthies who insist you must take a hacksaw to your own standard of living are themselves living very well. And they expect to continue to do so, thank you.

The whole ploy is such obvious hogwash that not even P. T. Barnum would have dared try to peddle it. Of course, times were different when he said there's a sucker born every minute. He didn't know they could be created even quicker—if the denizens of government, education, and the media were all in on the plot. We are *not* running out of energy.

But if the American people swallow the phony Rockefeller-inspired and financed propaganda, the doomsday prediction of depression and famine will be a self-fulfilling prophecy. If we can be panicked into surrendering our freedom in the name of survival, the socialist-fascist dictatorship of the Rockefellers' New World Order will be a reality.

Chapter Twelve
The Eternal Power Behind
the Throne

Single acts of tyranny may be ascribed to the accidental opinion of a day, but a series of oppressions, begun at a distinguished period, unalterable through every change of ministers, too plainly prove a deliberate, systematical plan of reducing us to slavery.

Thomas Jefferson

When John D. Rockefeller was coming close to monopolizing the oil industry, one of his favorite and most effective ploys was to capture a competitor from the inside. He would place his men inside a competitor's office, or bribe employees of other firms to do his bidding.

John D.'s descendants now play the same game with our government. It makes no difference which party is in power; whether a Democrat or Republican Administration, the Rockefeller people hold the key positions, especially in the fields of foreign policy and finance. The House of Rockefeller is the eternal power behind the throne.

Rockefeller influence in the White House began in 1894 with the election of William McKinley. But it was not until the election of Franklin Delano Roosevelt that it became a deciding factor in determining policy. In many ways, the New Deal was a Rockefeller deal.*

---

*Although it is generally believed that the New Deal was designed to help business and the stock market quickly recover from the depression, its effect was to prolong the depression for several years. We now know that this result was deliberately contrived; among other reasons, the Rockefellers wanted a depressed stock market so they could buy up shares cheaply. (It is worth noting that the "New Deal" dealt most kindly with the

The main Rockefeller agent was Harry Hopkins, who had been financed by the Rockefeller foundation for more than a decade when he ran the Organized Social Service. Hopkins was to become Franklin D. Roosevelt's *alter ego*, even to the point of living in the White House. He was the second most powerful man in America during the war years.

As Walter Winchell reported at the time, Hopkins acknowledged his debt to the Rockefellers when he was appointed Secretary of Commerce, by offering the post of Assistant Secretary to Nelson. William Rusher tells us in the *Los Angeles Herald Examiner* of September 7, 1975:

> Nelson Rockefeller was recruited for the New Deal by FDR's confidante, Harry Hopkins, back in the 1930's. . . . He apparently wasn't even a Republican by 1940, let along a conservative. In that year, at any rate, as World War II approached America, FDR did him the handsome favor of giving him a soft civilian berth in the White House where he remained straight through to V-J Day.

The fact that Nelson's name was number ten on the local draft board list, when he fortuitously "landed" his job with the New Deal, may explain why the young Rockefeller was so willing to abandon a plush family position to join the Washington bureaucracy.

The *New York Times* of May 20, 1960, reveals that after his appointment "Rockefeller became a Roosevelt intimate, spending secret holidays with the President at Shangri-la (now Camp David). . . ." Twenty years later, Nelson reminisced to *Newsweek* that "this country hasn't had a sense of purpose and direction since Roosevelt." In that 1962 interview, the future Vice President dismissed conservative Republicans, saying they were "like cattle that aren't going anywhere."

In the Dwight D. Eisenhower (CFR) Administration, Nelson helped to create and served as Assistant Secretary in the Department of Health, Education and Welfare,

---

Rockefeller interests. For detailed information see Chapter III of the author's book, *None Dare Call It Conspiracy*, and Antony Sutton's *Wall Street And F.D.R.*)

which now takes an even larger portion of the Federal Budget than does defense. But the job of running a government is so immense that the Rockefellers must delegate most of the work to friends, associates, hirelings and agents.

Eisenhower's first Secretary of State, John Foster Dulles (CFR), was a Rockefeller cousin. Dulles' successor was Christian Herter (CFR), who had the good sense to marry into the Standard Oil fortune. Herbert Brownell (CFR) was a Rockefeller employee when Eisenhower tapped him to be Attorney General. Brownell subsequently selected hundreds of federal judges, district attorneys, U.S. Marshals, and White House staffers. Seventeen other key figures at the top of the Eisenhower Administration were supplied by the Rockefellers' CFR.

Soon after his election as President, John F. Kennedy (CFR) followed Rocky's advice and named Dean Rusk of the CFR to be his Secretary of State. Rusk, whom Kennedy had never met, took a leave of absence as head of the Rockefeller Foundation to accept the post. Kennedy's appointment for Under Secretary of State was Chester Bowles, a fellow CFR member who has been a trustee of the Rockefeller Brothers Fund and a director of the Rockefeller Foundation. Democrat Kennedy then named Standard Oil executive Alexander Trowbridge (CFR) as Assistant Secretary of Commerce, and President Johnson later promoted him to Secretary of Commerce. President Kennedy also named Roswell Gilpatrick (CFR), a trustee of the Rockefeller Brothers Fund, as Deputy Secretary of Defense. Virtually every top position in the administration of JFK and LBJ was held by a member of the CFR.

Richard Nixon appointed Nelson Rockefeller's attorney John Mitchell as Attorney General, and Mitchell ran the President's campaign for re-election and became his chief advisor on domestic policy. Nixon's first Vice President was the ill-fated Spiro Agnew, who had been national chairman of the Rockefeller for President Committee in 1968 and an outspoken *opponent* of Nixon until Rocky approved his White House role.

Chief advisor to both Nixon and Ford on foreign policy, of course, is the ubiquitious Secretary of State, Henry Kissinger, who left a staff position with the CFR to join the Nixon Administration. For ten years Kissinger had been Nelson Rockefeller's personal foreign policy advisor. Altogether Richard Nixon staffed his Administration with over 115 CFR members. (The complete list is contained in the author's *Richard Nixon: The Man Behind The Mask*.) The vast majority of these remain in the Ford-Rockefeller (or is it vice-versa?) regime.

Years ago, Nelson Rockefeller reportedly demanded, and received, the privilege of naming his men to top administrative posts on all important Republican committees—including the vital National, Senatorial, Congressional, and Policy committees. The effect on the Republican Party is all too (perfectly) clear. It has been reliably estimated that over the years the Rockefellers have placed at least five thousand persons in important positions at the highest levels of the federal government. The Rockefeller influence and authority now runs the top Civil Service bureaucracy, thereby transcending the administrations of mere Republicans and Democrats.*

Having a big stake in an internationalist foreign policy, the Rockefellers always make sure that the Secretary of State and the Director of the Central Intelligence Agency (CIA) are "their boys". Marshall, Acheson, Dulles, Herter, Rusk and Kissinger have all labored to turn the backward Soviet Union into a creditable power to force the Great Merger, while at the same time fighting wars to make the world safe for Standard Oil. The CIA has served as the State Department's and Standard Oil's enforcement

---

*Indeed, Ford's most important early appointment was Edward Levi as Attorney General. Levi was the first Attorney General in modern history who had never met the President who appointed him. It is well known in Washington political circles that Levi, from the Rockefeller-endowed University of Chicago, and not a Republican, was Nelson's choice. The new Attorney General has a reputation of being about as conservative as Mao's Red Guard.

arm, destroying genuine anti-communist movements around the world.* (Chile seems to be the one exception. Apparently the Rockefellers did not care to lose their holdings in that nation.) The CIA was created and staffed by Rockefeller relative Allen Dulles.

American foreign policy has meant billions of dollars for the Rockefellers. It has been paid for in many cases by the blood of our soldiers and in every case by the sweat of our taxpayers. In his *Reminiscences* John D. Rockefeller informs us: "One of our greatest helpers has been the State Department in Washington. Our ambassadors and ministers and consuls have aided to push our way into new markets to the utmost corners of the world."

Washington reporter Jack Anderson put it this way in 1967: ". . . the State Department has often taken its policies right out of the executive suites of the oil companies. When Big Oil can't get what it wants in foreign countries, the State Department tries to get it for them. In many countries, the American Embassies function virtually as branch offices for the Oil combine . . . The State Department can be found almost always on the side of the 'seven sisters', as the oil giants are known inside the industry. . . ." The more things change, the more they remain the same.

Just as the Rockefellers make sure their *capos* are running "our" perenially disastrous foreign policy, you can

---

*The Rockefellers occasionally lose a property to nationalization—at least temporarily—through madcap coups, but such instances are remarkably rare. Here is where Rockefeller influence in the World Bank comes in handy. In *The Political Economics of International Oil*, Michael Tanzer admits that, although the World Bank favors active government participation in virtually every other area, oil is a major exception: ". . . the general policies of the Bank strongly tend to favor minimizing the public sector's role. . . . The World Bank too has refused to lend money for any government oil operations in underdeveloped countries. In addition, the Bank has also played an active, albeit subsurface, role in trying to dissuade underdeveloped countries from using their own capital for oil exploration. . . ."

bet your last devalued dollar that the Rockefeller Mafia controls the national and international money game.

The Rockefellers have made the Treasury Department virtually a branch of the Chase Manhattan Bank. Eisenhower's Secretary of the Treasury was Robert Anderson (CFR). Kennedy "switched" to Douglas Dillon (CFR and a trustee of the Rockefeller Brothers Fund). Henry Fowler (CFR) was the House of Rockefeller's rep heading the Treasury during the LBJ era. And in the year of our Ford, William Simon (CFR) runs the temple for the CFR money changers.

While Secretary of the Treasury is a significant position, chairman of the Federal Reserve Board is infinitely more important. The Federal Reserve is a mystery wrapped in an enigma for most Americans. Yet it is critical to the Rockefeller manipulations of the economy.

The Rockefellers were instrumental in creating the Federal Reserve System. It was designed at a secret meeting in 1910 at Jekyl Island off the coast of Georgia. Rockefeller agent Frank Vanderlip admitted many years later in his memoirs:

> Despite my views about the value to society of greater publicity for the affairs of corporations, there was an occasion, near the close of 1910, when I was as secretive—indeed as furtive—as any conspirator . . . I do not feel it is any exaggeration to speak of our secret expedition to Jekyl Island as the occasion of the actual conception of what eventually became the Federal Reserve System.

Out of the Jekyl Island meeting came the Monetary Commission Report and from it, the Aldrich Bill. Warburg had urged that the proposed legislation be designated simply, the "Federal Reserve System," but Aldrich insisted his name appear as the bill's chief sponsor. This proved to be a serious mistake; the legislation was so obviously a project of the international bankers that it could not be pushed through Congress.

A new strategy had to be devised. The Republican Party was too closely identified with Wall Street. The conspirators recognized that the only way to establish a central bank was to disguise the proposal, and have it promoted by Democrats as a means to strip Wall Street of its power!

The opportunity to do this came in 1912 when the Jekyl Island conspirators induced Teddy Roosevelt to run on a third party ticket to split the Republican vote. The result was that the underdog Democrat, Woodrow Wilson, won. Wilson paid off like a slot machine that has just rung up three bars.*

In order to support the fiction that the Federal Reserve Act was a "people's bill," the *Insider* financiers put up a smoke-screen of opposition to it. It was strictly a case of Br'er Rabbit begging not to be thrown into the briar patch. Both Aldrich and Vanderlip denounced what was actually their own bill. Nearly twenty-five years later, Frank Vanderlip admitted: "Now although the Aldrich Federal Reserve Plan was defeated when it bore the name Aldrich, nevertheless its essential points were all contained in the plan that finally was adopted."

Taking advantage of Congress' desire to adjourn for Christmas, the Federal Reserve Act was passed on December 22, 1913, by a vote of 298 to 60 in the House, and in the Senate by a majority of 43 to 25.

After the vote, Congressman Charles A. Lindberg Sr., father of the famous aviator, told Congress:

> This act establishes the most gigantic trust on earth . . .
> When the President signs this act the invisible government by the money power, proven to exist by the Money Trust investigation, will be legalized. . . .
> This is the Aldrich Bill in disguise. . . .
> The new law will create inflation whenever the trusts want inflation. . . .

The Federal Reserve Act was, and still is, hailed as a victory of "democracy" over the "money trust." Nothing could be further from the truth. The whole central bank

---

*A more comprehensive account of the creation and operation of the Federal Reserve is told in the author's book, *None Dare Call It Conspiracy*.

concept was engineered by the very group it was supposed to strip of power.

How powerful is our "central bank"? The Federal Reserve controls our money supply and interest rates, and thereby manipulates the entire economy—creating inflation or deflation, recession or boom, and sending the stock market up or down at will. The Federal Reserve is so powerful that Congressman Wright Patman, Chairman of the House Banking Committee, maintains:

> In the United States today we have in effect two governments ... We have the duly constituted Government ... Then we have an independent, uncontrolled and uncoordinated government in the Federal Reserve System, operating the money powers which are reserved to Congress by the Constitution.

Neither Presidents, Congressmen nor Secretaries of the Treasury direct the Federal Reserve. In the matters of money, the Federal Reserve directs them!

How successful has the Federal Reserve System been? It depends on your point of view. Since Woodrow Wilson took his oath of office, the national debt has skyrocketed from $1 billion to over $500 billion. Interest paid to the international bankers holding that debt is staggering; at $27 billion annually, it is now the third largest item in the Federal Budget. And it is climbing steeply, as inflation pushes up the interest rate on government bonds, while the government runs grotesque deficits every year.

Under the brilliant expertise of these Rockefeller-CFR money managers, the dollar has lost three-fourths of its purchasing power since 1940. And the pace is accelerating. Soon your paper dollar, now totally divorced from gold and silver by Rockefellers' agents, will not be worth a plugged nickel. It's all right for the Rockefellers, they don't have to live on a fixed income or a pension.

America is being set up today for another 1929 style debacle. To think that the Crash of 1929 was an accident or the result of stupidity defies all logic. The international bankers who promoted the inflationary policies and pushed the propaganda which pumped up the stock market represented too many generations of accumulated expertise to have blundered into the Great Depression. As Congressman Louis McFadden, Chairman of the House Banking and Currency Committee, commented:

> It [the Depression] was not accidental. It was a carefully contrived occurrence . . . The international bankers sought to bring about a condition of despair here so that they might emerge as rulers of us all.

It was the game of boom and bust, using economic crisis to consolidate political power at the top where it can be most easily controlled.

The major cause of the economic collapse was the deliberately created credit inflation by the Federal Reserve. In six years it had inflated the money supply by sixty-two percent, inducing market speculations and unwise investments by middle Americans who were being set up for a shearing. When the shearing came, the sheep took a realistic look at their economy and panicked. Optimism was replaced by economic despair; despair produced a willingness to accept a major expansion of government controls over the economy.

Now, the Rockefellers are sharpening their shears to give the sheep of the world another trimming. But this time may be the last time. In 1929, America was a long way from total government. The next depression will be used as the excuse for complete socialist-fascist controls at home and the creation of a World Superstate internationally.

Just as the Rockefellers use the Export-Import Bank as a tool to loot the capital and credit-starved American economy and its over-taxed citizenry, so they also use the UN's World Bank as yet another siphon in the U.S. Taxpayer's wallet.

A key lieutenant in fleecing American workers has been Eugene Black (CFR), a director of the Rockefeller's Chase Manhattan Bank. For fifteen years Black was (successively) executive director, president, and then chairman of the executive directors of the World Bank. It is an amazing ''coincidence'' how officers of the

Rockefeller's Chase Manhattan Bank keep turning up as officials of the World Bank.

The current head of the World Bank is the notorious Robert Strange McNamara, who did more than any American since Benedict Arnold to betray America's defenses. If you have not guessed that McNamara is a member of the CFR, you haven't been reading carefully enough. Not surprisingly, Mr. McNamara is eager to multiply the World Bank's loans to finance socialism. As he puts it: "The rich nations could easily contribute more than they have done to the poor nations." He continues:

> We in the U.S. can do far more to cure our own national problems. And just as we can do more to correct those conditions, so we can do more to contribute to the economic development of the developing nations. It's simply a question of getting a proper order of priorities.

And in line with CFR policy, McNamara is already pushing the World Bank to begin pumping out your money to the Communist bloc. As Chairman McNamara puts it: "We're quite willing to receive approaches by any Eastern European or other Communist bloc members not now members of the bank."

Through their Council on Foreign Relations, the Family Rockefeller has controlled the executive branch of government, especially the Departments of State and Treasury. Public opinion is manufactured by the CFR's ventriloquists in the mass media. But, Congress still plays a key role in governing the United States. The House of Rockefeller has formed two organizations specifically to influence Congress. They are Common Cause and the National Committee for an Effective Congress.

The National Committee for an Effective Congress was formed by Eleanor Roosevelt in 1948 to elect "progressive" (read fascist-socialist) Senators. The organization makes no pretense at being a grass-roots group. The average donation by the limousine liberals to the NCEC in 1972 was $13,000.

Members of the NCEC believe the selection of Congressmen is too important to be left to the local voters.

Since 1948 they have helped change the composition of Congress by passing the hat around Wall Street to ensure that "their kind" of Congressman was elected in Montana, Iowa, Tennessee and West Virginia. "Their kind" includes such ultra-liberals as Senators Hubert Humphrey, Birch Bayh, Alan Cranston, Frank Church, Clifford Case, Adlai Stevenson, Thomas Eagleton, and George McGovern—all of whom have been supported by the Wall Street internationalists of the NCEC; and all of whom can be counted on to vote for more and more fascist-socialist government.

In the past, the National Committee for an Effective Congress has concentrated on bankrolling compliant Senators. But in 1974, the megabuck liberals began financing "their kind" of candidates for the House of Representatives. During the election that year, the NCEC worked to eliminate opponents of the Rockefeller's "New World Order." The result was a mighty leap to the left in the House, as dozens of veteran Conservatives went down to defeat.

For the 1974 campaign, the NCEC hired professional campaign managers for 49 Democrat candidates around the country. Thirty-five of them won and promptly became the much heralded "Freshman Democratic Caucus."

Having eliminated most of the old-line Republicans, in 1976, according to the *Washington Post*'s David Broder, the NCEC will concentrate on electing Liberal Republicans who can work with Nelson Rockefeller. Candidates who convince the multi-millionaire internationalists of the National Committee for an Effective Congress that they are willing to represent them, rather than their constituents, can receive unlimited thousands of dollars. It will come in the form of "services"—free publicity from the mass media, free "research," free polling to determine the "image" which the candidate needs to project, free attacks on opponents, free mailings and literature on appropriate "issues." Above all, the candidate can expect free workers who will not only manage his campaign, but will proceed to manage *him* when he gets to Congress.

The Rockefeller front entrusted with the task of creating popular support for the *Insiders'* takeover is an organization called Common Cause. Common Cause masquerades as "the people's lobby," but nothing could be further from the truth.

Common Cause was launched in the early 1970's with all of the hoopla of a million-dollar advertising campaign planned by P. T. Barnum. Full-page newspaper ads and slick direct-mail pieces announced that something called Common Cause would be neither Republican nor Democrat, but a "people's lobby," representing all Americans against the "rich and powerful." It should be sued for false advertising.

Chairman of Common Cause is an establishmentarian with impressive credentials, John Gardner. As Secretary of the Department of Health, Education and Welfare in the mid-1960's, Gardner pushed federal money and programs at everything that moved. In the area of federalized health care alone, HEW programs initiated under Gardner included Medicare, Medicaid, federal staffing of community mental health centers, federal planning of public health services, and scores of other socialist-fascist programs costing billions. But Gardner now heads an Establishment-financed "people's lobby" to destroy the "special interests" dominating politics.

Of course no huckster worth his salt is anxious for the public to become aware of the sting. So John Gardner has removed a few of his more revealing credits from the biography he prepares for *Who's Who In America*. Among those positions which he has expunged from the record are his seat on the board of trustees of the Rockefeller Brothers Fund. After all, it might be embarrassing while calling publicly for emasculating the power of the big banks and their fat trusts if people found out you are currently serving at the pleasure of the controllers of Chase Manhattan Bank. Some suspicious souls might doubt your sincerity. The giant oil producers are another "target" of Gardner's Common Cause. Naturally he no longer lists his position on the board of directors of

Shell Oil, which is the world's second-largest oil company.

Buried deep in the records of the Senate Clerk is a lobbyist's report filed by Gardner showing receipts for the last quarter of 1970. The largest donor was John D. Rockefeller III, who anted up twenty-five thousand dollars; David Rockefeller gave ten thousand dollars; Martha Rockefeller provided another ten thousand; Chase Manhattan Bank gave five thousand dollars; kindly Amory Houghton Jr. of the Rockefeller Foundation provided ten thousand; Nelson Rockefeller gave a guarded five hundred dollars; J. Richardson Dilworth, the family's financial advisor, gave five hundred; A. Meyer, senior partner in Lazard Freres and Company, the Rothschild's U.S. Bank, provided ten thousand dollars; A. E. Friedman, a partner in the Rockefeller-allied Kuhn, Loeb and Company, gave a thousand; and, the list of the Establishment's super-rich goes on and on and on.

Notice that this was the "up-front" money—the big cash that made Common Cause possible. It was the Rockefellers and their allies who supplied the seed money, the money used to buy the advertisements in all those magazines and newspapers and to pay for the mailing to 2.5 million Americans soliciting those fifteen-dollar memberships in Common Cause. Without the Rockefellers there would have been no kickoff, no quarter of a million members whose dues allow the organization's spokesmen to claim that the Rockefellers supplied only a small percentage of money raised. But how many people out in Kumquat Corners would fall for the Gardner snake oil routine if they knew that he was fronting for Daddy Rockabucks? About as many as as attend submarine races at Boise.

Common Cause claims a membership of 350,000 and operates on an annual budget of $6.3 million. Ironically, in the yearly report required by law of lobbyists it now finds itself in the position of declaring the highest expenditures of any lobby on Capitol Hill. The Rockefeller anti-lobby is now the biggest of the bunch.

The massive coverage given Common Cause by the

Establishment journals is indicated by the fact that during 1974 the New York Times News Service, alone, carried over one hundred articles about Common Cause. That is a major article about Common Cause every 3.5 days. When you consider the hundreds of key newspapers across the country that subscribe to the New York Times News Service, and remember that the other major news services have also carried a similarly large number of stories puffing Common Cause, you readily see why the impact of its every move is enormous.

The other major triumph of the Rockefellers' Common Cause is the "campaign reform" act of 1974. In its recruiting brochure, Common Cause proclaims that "members of Common Cause have led the citizens' effort to change the way our nation finances political campaigns."

There are many dangerous implications to the law. Howard Phillips reports in *Human Events* for November 2, 1974, that under this legislation "a candidate whose views are at variance from the dominant political establishment is limited in how much he may spend or cause to be expended in his own behalf." Meanwhile, Phillips says, the problems of candidates challenging the Liberal Establishment "can be seriously increased through 'non-political expenditures made by issue-oriented' Liberal organizations [like NCEC or Common Cause] which put forth large sums to advance their viewpoints, although escaping any spending limitations under the act (because, technically, the money is not spent 'against' the candidate with which they disagree)."

This is what Common Cause calls "opening up the system." It is a dodge to allow the Rockefellers and their friends who control Common Cause to raise and spend vast sums to defeat their opponents while limiting the ability of those opponents to raise funds.

Now that the Rockefellers have the kind of Congress they want, they mean to keep it that way. They know that a Liberal Establishment which controls the mass media can give its favorite candidate vast amounts of free publicity which, in the past, anti-Establishment candidates could only match with money. They believe that they have now closed that potential source of opposition.

Common Cause advertises that it is a "new force on the American political scene." What it is . . . is a Rockefeller political front. And it is dangerously powerful. As Congressman F. Edward Hebert declared in an NBC interview on February 5, 1975:

> The American people better wake up to what this outfit is doing because they can destroy the country. The new Congressmen are not running Congress, Common Cause is running Congress. Who elected them?

That is a good question, Congressman Hebert. And the answer is: The same *Insiders* who "elected" Nelson Rockefeller Vice President of the United States.

The Watergate Caper, the *coup d'etat* that knocked President Nixon out of the White House, was carefully engineered by the two agents for the House of Rockefeller shown above. It is now known that Henry Kissinger (left) was responsible for creating the Plumbers squad in the first place, while the "instant General," Alexander Haig (right), made sure that the most incriminating evidence on the tapes was given in advance to the men investigating his boss! Together, the two men forced a bitter and dejected Nixon to resign, thus paving the way (finally!) to get a Rockefeller into the White House—without risking an election Rocky would surely lose.

Chapter Thirteen
Was Nixon Watergated?

After all, when you think of what I had, what else [other than the Presidency] was there to aspire to?

Nelson Rockefeller

Nelson Rockefeller has admitted that his goal in life since he was a child has been to be President of the United States. "After all," he admitted, "when you think of what I had, what else was there to aspire to?" He has a point there.

Newsweek of September 2, 1974 tells us: "Ever since his boyhood meeting with Teddy Roosevelt, it seems, Nelson Rockefeller had been propelling himself toward the Oval Office. Nothing less would suit his ambition. . . ."

But the road to the White House for Nelson has been, if you will pardon the expression, rocky. He has had to settle for an unelected and politically engineered Vice Presidency, a position at which he had previously turned up his nose several times.

Nelson's first attempt at the Presidency came in 1960, shortly after his election as governor of New York. Richard Nixon had been Vice President for eight years, however, and had spent much of the time making speeches for the GOP. In 1960, he collected his political IOUs from the majority of party activists and Rockefeller had no chance of getting the nomination. When Rocky found he could not win the actual nomination, he moved to dictate policy from behind the scenes. A meeting was thus arranged between Rockefeller and Nixon on the Saturday before the Republican Convention opened in Chicago.

The Republican Platform Committee had been meeting for an entire week, laboriously pounding out a platform reflecting the views of party members from all fifty states.

But, at the meeting between Nixon and Nelson at Rockefeller's Fifth Avenue apartment in New York City, Nixon accepted everything Rockefeller dictated. The Platform Committee's sweat-stained document was ashcanned and, presto Chicago, Rockefeller's Liberal platform was substituted. Goldwater dejectedly called Nixon's surrender to Rockefeller "the Munich of the Republican Party."

Republicans everywhere understood the significance of the new Rockefeller-Nixon alliance. Nixon had traded his independence for approval by the House of Rockefeller.

The truth is that Nixon had the nomination in the bag; there was no need for him to crawl to Rockefeller to win it. Nixon knew this, but he also knew who held the ultimate power behind both political parties.

Certainly there was never any love lost between Richard and Rocky. They have detested each other for years. *Newsweek* of September 2, 1974, tells us: "The Nixon Presidency was a painful period for the proud governor. Privately, friends say, Rockefeller despised the self-made man from Yorba Linda. . . ."

Rocky, the man born to economic royalty, must have deeply resented having to operate through this Sammy Glick-type character who looked like a used car salesman, but had clawed his way to the White House. But the two men needed each other. Nelson's influence in the GOP is immense at the top, but is almost non-existent among voters at the grass roots.

After forcing Nixon's humiliating surrender, Rockefeller virtually sat out the 1960 campaign and allowed New York to go for Kennedy. Nixon surprised most observers by quietly accepting the defeat that had been arranged for him, refusing even to protest the vote fraud in Texas and Illinois which deprived him of the election.*

Richard Nixon returned to California to practice law but remained at the beck and call of his jealous and hostile boss in New York. One indication of their real relationship was the Joe Shell affair. Shell was a long-time Cali-

---

*This story is described at length in *Richard Nixon: The Man Behind The Mask* by this author.

fornia State Assemblyman who planned to oppose Democrat incumbent Pat Brown for the governorship in 1962. Early in the year, he received a call from Rockefeller, asking whom he would support at the 1964 convention if he were elected. The conservative Assemblyman told Rockefeller that under no circumstances could he support the ultra-liberal New Yorker. One week later, Shell's office received a call from Rockefeller's New York office with the news that Richard Nixon would oppose Shell in the GOP gubernatorial primary—even though Nixon had previously assured Shell that he had absolutely no interest in being Governor of California.

The important point here is that Nixon was not interested in the job until he received orders from his boss in New York. Nixon had everything to lose and virtually nothing to gain by running against an incumbent Democrat governor in a state with an overwhelming Democrat registration plurality.

Following an incredibly inept campaign, in which his chief target was Nelson's old bugaboo, the "radical right," not Bungling Brown's record, Nixon lost the race. His political career appeared to have come to an end. As he put it: "You won't have Nixon to kick around anymore."

Apparently, the Nixon candidacy was as much a test of obedience as it was a move to head off a potential Rockefeller opponent. In any case, having thrown himself onto a bed of nails at the behest of Rockefeller, Nixon was thrown a lifeline and brought to New York. He moved into an elegant $125,000 apartment in the same building as Nelson Rockefeller—the very one in which the infamous "Compact of Fifth Avenue" was signed. Nixon was made a partner in a law firm which did a lot of trust and bond business with the friendly folk at Chase Manhattan Bank.

During the next five years Nixon practiced very little law, yet his net worth jumped from practically nothing to over half-a-million dollars. Most of his time was spent touring the nation and the world rebuilding his political reputation. When the Rockefellers needed him in 1968, he had been resurrected from the political trash heap and turned into a legitimate candidate.

Meanwhile, Nelson had been giving the Presidency the old college try himself. He might have made it in 1964 had not his divorce and remarriage alienated a large segment of middle America. Rockefeller learned the hard way that a lot of women don't forgive a man who abandons a wife of long standing to marry a much younger and prettier one. When the new bride abandons her own children to marry the man in question, it compounds the outrage.

In 1968, Nelson made a half-hearted attempt to wrest the nomination from Nixon. But the handwriting was on the wailing wall. "The old avidity is gone," groaned Nelson. Once again, he had to settle for owning the team instead of starting as quarterback.

Nixon's appointments to policy-making positions confirmed that the House of Rockefeller did indeed own the team: they went almost entirely to Rockefeller men. In his inner circle, however, Nixon tried to surround himself with men like H. R. Haldeman and John Ehrlichman, who were personally loyal to him, not to Rockefeller. The two most notable exceptions were Kissinger and General Alexander Haig. Both men were known Rockefeller agents, and it is these two men who may have masterminded Nixon's early retirement.

If Nixon was an obedient Rockefeller man—if not necessarily a loyal one—why then did the Rockefeller-controlled media orchestrate the campaign to dispose him? Several possible explanations have been advanced. One is that Nixon grew too accustomed to the prerogatives of power, and believed that he had become an equal partner in the deal. There are some hints that Nixon himself may have initiated some of the in-fighting between the two factions. The forced resignation of Spiro Agnew, brought about by a combination of pressure from the Executive Branch and prosecution by Executive departments, may have been part of this.

Another suggestion is that Rockefeller gave the nudge that toppled Agnew from the White House, counting on

Nixon to appoint him to the Vice Presidency. When Nixon refused, and appointed Ford instead, the media dropped on him like a piano from the top of a ten-story building.

We may never know the full story of what started the internecine warfare. But we do know what was the decisive encounter in the battle: Watergate. And as we unravel the twisting threads of this strange saga, we find that each tug that ultimately toppled Nixon from the throne can be traced to Rockefeller.

The burglary at the Democratic Headquarters in the Watergate Hotel was not exactly carried out with the precision of a James Bond movie. It was more like the Three Stooges at their most slapstick. It was so clumsy, in fact, that the whole operation smells of a set-up. First: one of the burglars alerted a guard, by replacing the tape over the door locks after the guard had discovered and removed the first one. Even though their efforts had been discovered, the boss of the operation, Gordon Liddy, sent the burglars back to the Watergate. There they proceeded to flash lights, rip the place apart, and in general act as if they had all night to perform their mission. The man posted as lookout saw the police enter the building, but either failed to alert the men inside—or his warning was ignored.

It was as though the burglars were *meant* to be caught. And when they were, one of them conveniently was carrying the White House telephone number of E. Howard Hunt in his pocket.

Watergate began with the creation of the "Plumbers." The Plumbers were created by Kissinger to stop leaks on his staff. Both Nixon staffers John Dean and Charles Colson reported that Kissinger got Nixon so upset over leaks that the President decided, *at Kissinger's suggestion*, to set up a Special White House Investigating Unit, which later became known as the Plumbers. According to Dean, it was Rockefeller who had Kissinger sucker Nixon into forming the Plumbers. Little did Nixon know that he was being mousetrapped.

Nationally syndicated columnist Paul Scott reports:

Records of the Senate Watergate Committee

investigation indicates that Dean's testimony concerning Rockefeller was never followed up by the committee's staff. The reason: Committee members were against calling Rockefeller.

Kissinger put a member of his staff, David Young, in charge of the unit. You have never heard of David Young? Join the multitudes. He was a Wall Street lawyer who had worked for Rockefeller before being promoted to Kissinger's staff. After Watergate, Young was spirited off to a cushy assignment in London as a very advanced student, and the mediacracy has dutifully ignored his key role in Watergate.

The Watergate burglary, which was bungled more badly than a Keystone Cops chase, ended with a proven link to the White House. But no one ever claimed that Nixon gave the nod for the break-in; it was his role in the coverup that led to his downfall.

Watergate did start in the White House, however. But not by Nixon or any of his men. It was launched by the premier Rockefeller man, Henry Kissinger.

It was the activities of the Plumbers which brought the downfall of Richard Nixon. And Kissinger, Rockefeller and the CIA were obviously deeply involved. Former White House aide Charles Colson has said that Nixon suspected the CIA was in the plot "up to their eyeballs." Colson says Nixon wanted to fire the director of the CIA and personally investigate what was believed to be a CIA conspiracy against him. He was persuaded not to do so by General Alexander Haig, the Rockefeller man who replaced Bob Haldeman. Colson portrays Nixon as a virtual captive of Kissinger and Haig in the Oval Office during his last months in the Presidency.

But Richard Nixon would have survived the Watergate scandal had it not been for *those damned tapes*. At the beginning of the Watergate hearings, no one even knew they existed. The fact that all Nixon conversations had been recorded was revealed almost casually by Alexander Butterfield, White House liaison with the Secret Service. It is hard to believe that this bombshell, which was to remove a President, could be dropped with such an air of innocence. Could it have been planned?

We now know that Butterfield had been a CIA informant. He has been accused of working with (if not for) the CIA when he was in charge of all the tapings in the White House. Had Blabbermouth Butterfield, who was called to testify about other matters—not the tapes—"stonewalled" it, Nixon would not have been forced to resign. Even if asked a direct question about any recordings, Butterfield could have maintained that such matters related to national security and must remain confidential.

Nixon has said that the taping system was installed in the Oval Room at the suggestion of LBJ to preserve his conversations for posterity. Soon the whole White House and even Camp David were bugged. The White House monitoring system kept better track of people than do most prisons. The President could not walk from one room to another without that fact being recorded and a buzzer ringing and a light flashing on a console operated by Butterfield. Voices automatically started the tape recorders spinning. Keep in mind that it was not Mr. Nixon who turned the recorders off and on. It is as though the President were under constant surveillance by others, who wanted to know about his every word and movement.

Why didn't Nixon have the tape machines shut off the day after the Watergate arrests? Or, failing that, why didn't he destroy the tapes after Butterfield revealed their existence? Several rationalizations have been put forth, none of which ring true. One is that Nixon was mesmerized by the arrogance of power and did not believe the Supreme Court could or would subpoena the tapes. Since there was no precedent, why take the risk? Nixon must have known his very survival as President of the United States was at stake.

Another explanation is that Nixon is compulsively greedy for money and wanted to keep the tapes for use in writing his memoirs, or to donate to the national archives and take a multimillion dollar tax deduction. Much as

Nixon may like money, he would hardly jeopardize the Presidency—and risk a jail term—to keep the tapes. And he is now in the process of writing his memoirs for a million-dollar fee without benefit of those tapes.

Remember, releasing the tapes would not exonerate Nixon, they would prove him guilty of every cover-up charge made against him. Why would this cunning politician, this ruthless abuser of power, this man from whom no one would buy a used car, not simply destroy the tapes himself?

Nixon could have gone on national television in the great tradition of the Checkers speech, and said something like this:

> My fellow Americans. As your President, it is my sacred duty to protect your rights and our national security. And, let me make this perfectly clear—I shall not shrink from that duty, no matter how unpleasant the consequences.
>
> The tapes contained privileged and highly secret information, the publication of which would embarass many honorable public servants and jeopardize our delicate relations with foreign powers. It is therefore necessary to do what is best for the country and not what is best for myself.
>
> Public release of the tapes would exonerate me, but jeopardize the fate of the nation. I have met this obligation, knowing full well that I shall be terribly criticized by a cynical and hostile press, by destroying the tapes. I know that you, the American people—the finest people in the world—will back me up in this crisis. Thank you and good night.

To be sure, if Nixon had "stonewalled" it this way, the screaming would have been loud and profane. Senator Kennedy, the hero of Chappaquiddick, would have made a speech about abusing power to cover up crimes. But, *there would have been no proof.* And there is no way in the world that the President of the United States could have been removed from office without such evidence. Controversy would rage and Nixon would finish his second term under a cloud of doubt. But, there is no doubt he would finish the term! Better ugly suspicions than the damning truth. Watergate Prosecutor Leon Jaworski has admitted that "if Mr. Nixon had destroyed the tapes at the time their existence was disclosed in July, 1973, he would still be President."

Can anybody believe, as Dr. Susan Huck has asked, that Nixon sat there like a good scout, watching the lynch mob fasten a hangman's knot out of those wretched tapes, and refuse to destroy the noose? That isn't the Nixon depicted on the tapes—much less in public life.

Why then did not Nixon, that ultimate political opportunist, burn the tapes? We believe the only logical answer is that either Nixon did not control the tapes, or he knew there was more than one set. In a word, he did not destroy them because he could not.

Have you ever wondered how *everybody* seemed to know what was on the tapes, and *where*, before they were "turned over" to committee staffs, special prosecutors, or Judge Sirica? The mediacracy didn't wonder. So far as we can discover, the only person who has asked this question is Dr. Susan Huck, in the February 1975 issue of *American Opinion* magazine.

Consider the fantastic detail involved in the requests. On August 14th, for example, Judge Sirica demanded the "entire segment of tape on the reel identified as 'White House telephone start 5/25/72 (2:00 P.M.) (skipping 8 lines) 6/23/72 (2:50 P.M.) (832) complete.'" I don't know what all the identifying numbers mean—but you have to agree that only somebody very familiar with the tapes *would* know. These boys knew *precisely* what to look for! Here is another sample request:

> January 8, 1973 from 4:05 to 5:34 P.M. (E.O.B.)
> a) at approximately 10 minutes and 15 seconds into the conversation, a segment lasting 6 minutes and 31 seconds:
> b) at approximately 67 minutes into the conversation, a segment lasting 11 minutes;
> c) at approximately 82 minutes and 15 seconds into the conversation, a segment lasting 5 minutes and 31 seconds.

As Dr. Huck observed: "It does sound as though somebody—obviously not the President—has been curled up with those tapes for many a long hour, doesn't it? Somebody knows exactly where the juicy parts are, down to the second."

Remember, all White House conversations—in person and on the phone—had been "bugged" for at least a year. There were literally miles of tapes in storage somewhere. But it is obvious the investigators *already had the evidence they sought* when the various subpoenas were issued!

Who then controlled the tapes, or had access to a duplicate set? There is (understandably) very little information available on this crucial question. It is worth noting, however, that while LBJ's recording system had been installed by the Army Signal Corps, the Nixon monitors were established by the Secret Service. So it is of more than passing significance that *Newsweek* on September 23, 1974, reported:

> While former White House chief of staff H. R. Haldeman awaits trial for his part in Watergate, the Secret Service chief he ousted from the White House last year has landed a plum job. Robert H. Taylor, 49, who tangled with Haldeman over Nixon security procedures, is now head of the private security forces for all the far-flung Rockefeller family enterprises.

Hmmm. Once Nixon is deposed, the head of the Secret Service—the man in charge of the agency which was in charge of the tapes—gets "a plum job" with the Rockefeller Empire. And what of the Rockefeller's number one man in the White House?

We know that Henry Kissinger was deeply involved in wiretapping his own staff and several journalists. But the one member of the White House staff who apparently *never* had his remarks taped in the Oval Office was Herr Kissinger—who also, as it happens, was chief of *all* U.S. intelligence gathering operations. And who also, we now know, was responsible for establishing the Plumbers in the first place!

But through all of this, Kissinger's loyalty was not with his President, it was with the Rockefellers! Kissinger had been through three losing campaigns with Nelson Rockefeller and openly spoke of despising Nixon. Biographer David Hanna quotes Kissinger as stating, after Nixon's nomination in 1968: "That man is unfit to be President. I would never work for that man. He is a disaster." Yet Kissinger was the *first* appointment made by Nixon.

Nixon did not know Kissinger well; in fact, he had only met the man once before in his life—at a cocktail party. And Kissinger was on record as standing 180 degrees to the left of Nixon's campaign utterances. Clearly, Kissinger was put in the Nixon Administration by Rockefeller (who sent his protege off to Washington with a tidy little gift of $50,000). In his Vice Presidential hearings, Nelson Rockefeller even acknowledged that Kissinger took the job because Rocky asked him to do so.*

While it was Henry Kissinger who set Nixon's head on the chopping block, it was another Rockefeller agent, General Alexander Haig, who applied the axe. Haig was appointed—at Kissinger's suggestion—as an interim replacement for the hastily deposed Bob Haldeman.

Like Dwight Eisenhower and George Marshall, two generals whose careers had a bad case of the blahs until anointed by the House of Rockefeller, Haig's career took off like a Saturn rocket when he joined the Rockefeller team through the Council on Foreign Relations. In 1969, he was a colonel. Four years later he had miraculously become a four star general, having skipped the three star rank entirely. What happened to trigger this remarkable rise? In 1969, Haig became an assistant to Kissinger; subsequently, he was catapulted over 240 general officers when Nixon raised him to four-star rank. Such a promotion should mark Haig as one of the great military leaders in our history. But, his promotions did not come as

---

*So critical was the Kissinger appointment that Nixon waived the customary FBI security clearance for his nominee as Secretary of State. The reasons Kissinger could never pass accurate security procedures will be discussed in our follow-up book, *The Kissinger File.*

a result of military achievements—there were none. They were political. Haig was now a general in the Rockefeller Army, an army which tells other armies when to march.

Syndicated columnist Jerald TerHorst, who did a short stint as Ford's press secretary, tells us:

> For most of the final Nixon year, as Haig himself would agree, he [Haig] was the acting president of the United States. With a troubled President drawing more and more within his shell, everyone in the government, with the possible exception of [Haig's sponsor] Kissinger, was working for Al Haig.

William Safire, a Nixon speech writer, says in the November 11, 1973 *New York Times* magazine: "Haig is far more powerful than Haldeman ever was; but he exercises it more gently . . . Haig learned this technique from the past master, Henry Kissinger. . . ." In his new book, *Before The Fall*, Safire calls Haig "Kissinger's alter ego." Significantly, the *Washington Post's* Barry Sussman refers to Haig as "Butterfield's former colleague."

You see, it was Alexander Haig who had control of the vault where the Watergate tapes were kept. Two months after Haig became the keeper of the keys, his former colleague Butterfield tipped off the Watergate Committee about their existence. Since it is perfectly clear that the subpoenas for the tapes were written by persons already possessing a detailed familiarity with their contents, it is painfully obvious that Haig had *already* provided them with copies of the pertinent excerpts.

It was now time for the axe to fall. In the June 8, 1975 issue of *Parade* magazine, Lloyd Shearer tells us: "From May 1973 to August 1974, Haig was Nixon's chief of staff. It was he who adroitly engineered, orchestrated and choreographed Nixon's resignation from the Presidency."

According to Shearer, Nixon was determined not to resign. "Yet Haig knew that he must." The reason for Haig's insistence, according to *Parade*, was that if the President insisted on a trial *and lost*, he would lose his pension and other government benefits. You will pardon us for believing that Haig had *much* more compelling reasons for giving Nixon the final push.

How did he do it? Haig "orchestrated the resignation march," says Shearer, by taking the evidence against Nixon to Republican Congressmen, Presidential speech writers and others close to Nixon. "Haig saw to it that Senator Barry Goldwater, the conservative bulwark of the Republican Party, was provided with the damning tape transcripts of June 23," Shearer reported. Get that? The President's chief assistant finds out the boss won't budge, so he takes copies of the most damning tapes to the few supporters Nixon had left! Why didn't Nixon fire Haig *and* burn the tapes? Again, the most obvious, most logical answer is that he did not because he could not.

Shearer continues:

> And at the next and final Cabinet meeting, with at least half the members expecting him to resign, Nixon rambled on about inflation, declared his intention to stay on, ordered them to pass the word.
> Haig and Kissinger exchanged glances. ! When the Cabinet meeting was over, Kissinger stayed behind. Gently he suggested that the President resign.

Later that same afternoon, "Haig played his final card." Republican Senate leaders Hugh Scott and Barry Goldwater, joined by House Minority Leader John Rhodes, visited Nixon and told him his support in the Senate had evaporated. "That night," reports Shearer, "after again talking to Kissinger and Haig, Richard Nixon decided to resign."

And that is how the Three Muskateers for the House of Rockefeller engineered the *coup d'etat* that removed Nixon from the White House, and put Nelson in. There must have been *quite* a celebration that night in Pocantico Hills.

Please do not misunderstand us. We are not claiming that Richard Nixon was an innocent lamb done in by the big bad wolf. It was more like Al Capone rubbing out Bugs Moran and then sending flowers to the funeral. The point is that the entire scenerio—from the creation of the

Plumbers, through the incredibly bungled Watergate break-in, to the revelation of the existence of the tapes, to the preservation of the tapes and their use to force Nixon to resign—was written and directed by Rockefeller front men.

It is not without meaning that only those connected with the Rockefeller empire survived Watergate, while nearly everybody else was in disgrace—some pounding big rocks into little rocks.

Alexander Haig, the "instant General" as Dr. Huck called him, was quick to get his reward. Haig is now Supreme Allied Commander Europe, the general in charge of the NATO military command. In order to replace Haldeman, Haig had to retire from the Army. Can you imagine chucking four stars for a ride on the *Titanic*? Not bloody likely. There can be little doubt that Haig had been promised instant reinstatement and a very posh life jacket when the good ship *Nixonia* slipped beneath the waves. He got both.

Henry Kissinger is another big Watergate winner. Despite the fact that he not only bugged his own staff, but newspaper reporters as well, nary a word of criticism appeared in the press. Then came the disclosure that Kissinger was responsible for creating the Plumbers. Ho hum. During the Watergate scandals, Kissinger rose to the high office of Secretary of State while retaining his position as National Security Advisor. He had unprecedented power over foreign policy and intelligence. The source of his power was his sponsor, Nelson Rockefeller.

Kissinger proved, once again, that no man can serve two masters. Just as Haig had said that he "was never a Nixon man," Kissinger had boasted of Nixon, "I would never work for that man." He didn't. He worked for the Rockefellers.

Another beneficiary of the Watergate fiasco was that "staunch mid-western conservative," Gerald Ford. As usual, the image created by the media moguls and the truth are light years apart. Despite what some wags have said, Ford showed, while serving on the Warren Commission investigating the assassination of John F. Kennedy, that he had *not* played football without a helmet once too often: he proved he could keep his mouth shut about a major cover-up. At the time he was made Vice President, Ford had attended Bilderberger meetings and had been appointed by Rockefeller to the National Commission on Critical Choices.*

The catalyst who arranged Ford's appointment was former Wisconsin Congressman Mel Laird. Laird had been Secretary of Defense under Nixon and later a Presidential advisor. A member of Rockefeller's CFR, Laird knows where the power lies. If you will pardon the pun, he keeps his standards well oiled.

Acting as what Paul Scott calls "Mr. Inside" for Rockefeller, Laird succeeded in talking Nixon out of nominating former Treasury Secretary John Connally to succeed Agnew. He convinced the President that Connally could never be confirmed by Congress and suggested the compromise nomination of Gerald Ford as Vice President.

But of course, the ultimate winner of the Watergate roulette was Nelson Rockefeller. He is now only the proverbial heartbeat away from his lifelong ambition—to be President of these United States. (And just recently, two women have pointed pistols at jovial Jerry and his limousine was in an automobile accident. Understandably, Jerry doesn't look quite so merry anymore.)

When Bobo Sears Rockefeller was obtaining a divorce from the late Winthrop Rockefeller, she exploded two bombshells at the trial. The first was that Winthrop had one of the largest and most valuable collections of pornography in the world. (The punch line is that the pictures were not of girls.)

---

*The Bilderbergers are sort of an international CFR. They meet once a year at some posh secluded hideaway to make a mockery of democracy. The meetings, composed of the world's elite men of politics, business, banking and labor, receive virtually no serious attention from the mediacracy. See Chapter 5 of *None Dare Call It Conspiracy*.

Revelation number two from the bizarre divorce proceedings was the disclosure that the Brothers Rockefeller would get together from time to time—to brainstorm on ways they could make Nelson the President, without the benefit of an election. (They realized he could never get into the Oval Office via the ballot box.)

So Rockefeller became an *appointed* Vice President. And, he was named by a man who was not elected, who was appointed by a man who resigned because he was about to be impeached. We doubt if the Brothers Rockefeller could dream up anything quite this wild even after the fifth martini. Or could they?

Ford went through the motions of asking Republican Congressional leaders for their recommendations for the Vice Presidency. The choice had all the suspense of an election in Russia. Anybody who was surprised at the selection of Rockefeller must have arrived in town on top of a wagon full of turnips.

Are we suggesting there was a deal made for Nixon to appoint Ford, get pardoned by the new President, and then have Ford select Nelson Rockefeller as Vice President? That is *exactly* what we are saying. Anyone who doubts such a deal was made probably thinks professional wrestling matches are for real. It may just be coincidental, but on December 7, 1973, the headline on the upper-right-hand part of page one of the *New York Times* was: FORD SWORN AS VICE-PRESIDENT AFTER HOUSE APPROVES. The upper-left-hand headline of the very same issue read: GOVERNOR TO QUIT AND SEEK PRESIDENCY, HIS AIDES SAY.

While the nation focused on the Watergate hearings circus, the real show was going on inside a different tent. Columnist Paul Scott wrote at the time: "The drama-packed Senate Watergate hearings are only the colorful sideshow to one of the boldest and slickest transfers in U.S. history." And he continued with this revelation:

With everyone's attention focused on the cast of "small time" actors parading before the TV cameras recording the special Senate inquiry, only a few privileged insiders are alert to the really big show taking place at the other end of Pennsylvania Avenue.

As part of the plan to create a new world order [world government], the main show involves the carefully planned transfer of power from President Nixon to New York's Governor Rockefeller, now strategically positioning himself to become the President's heir apparent for 1976.

Whether Rockefeller with his family's vast economic wealth, social and political power will be able to pull off this carefully managed "power grab" is one of the most chilling and exciting political stories unfolding in our times."

Half of the Rockefeller *coup d'etat* has already been achieved. The question of the decade is: Where does Rocky go now? In 1968, after his third flop on the primary circuit, Rocky announced: ". . . the old avidity is gone." Has the "old avidity" returned? Is a four-pound robin fat? Does King Kong like bananas? Obviously the Rockefellers did not go to all of the trouble in setting the Watergate wheels in motion without having something big in mind.

Being a political prognosticator is an occupation only slightly less dangerous than riding tandem with Evel Knievel. Gathering facts is one thing, projecting them with accuracy into the future is quite another. Circumstances change, and we don't think there is a single plan which has been carved in stone. The Rockefellers never put all of their financial or political eggs in one basket. Doubtless, the family is considering a whole fleet of alternatives.

Rocky now says that he will not run with Ford in '76. He did not say he wouldn't run without him. Our Washington sources tell us that it was Nelson's idea to announce that he would not be on a Ford ticket, and that Jerry unmerrily begged him not to make the announcement. The reason Nelson is getting off the S.S. Jerry Ford, is that it is a sinking ship. Rocky's private polls reportedly show that Ford could well lose early '76 primaries and thereby throw the nomination wide open.

At that point the Rockefeller bandwagon would begin rolling with the greatest media promotion campaign in history, the theme being that only Rocky can save us. Indeed, according to Washington's best informed columnist, Paul Scott, Rockefeller began setting up an independent campaign organization two weeks before announcing he would not run with Ford. But wait, the plot thickens.

Many will refuse to believe the next prediction will happen, but we would bet our last farthing on it. If Nelson gets the top spot, the number two man on the ticket will be Ronald Reagan. It will be successfully sold to the Republican faithful across the nation as "the ticket to save the party." Would Reagan prostitute himself to accept the number two man on a Rocky ticket? Unfortunately, the answer is yes. Reagan will do whatever his "Kitchen Cabinet" of money men tell him to do. When he first got the Republican nomination for the Governorship of California in 1966, he quickly cut himself loose from tough conservatives and put Rockefeller men in as his key advisors.

Whether Rocky is at the top or in the number two position on the ticket may depend on whether his private surveys indicate he could be elected President. Recent public polls show that he is not exactly as popular with the American people as ice cream at a picnic. Even though the Rockefeller family is reportedly ready to spend $100 million dollars to put Nelson in the White House, it still might not work. The American people seem intuitively suspicious of him. How widely this book is read could influence Rocky's decision.

In addition to financing a lavish direct and indirect campaign for a Rockefeller-Reagan ticket, the House of Rockefeller can be counted upon to pump money in a thousand different and devious ways into splitting the Democrat vote. The odds-on favorite to get the Democrat nod is Hubert Humphrey. The U.S. has moved so far toward fascism-socialism that Hubert Humphrey, a founder of the radical Americans for Democratic Action

(ADA), is now considered to be a middle-of-the-road candidate. Like Nixon in 1968, Humphrey is a man whose time has come. Nobody is too wild about him, but he is acceptable to most.

A far left ticket headed by Eugene McCarthy or Senator Frank Church of Idaho would siphon off enough traditional Democrats so that the Republicans could win with forty percent of the vote. Divide and conquer is the name of the electoral game.

Wallace can be counted upon to run as a patriotic third party candidate and take some workingman-type votes away from Humphrey. Wallace is not a Rockefeller man and the family would hope that he does not start such a wildfire rebellion against the Establishment that he actually gets elected.

Meanwhile Nelson can continue as the *de facto* President, letting Ford walk around with a target on his back. Since Ford has made Rocky head of the Domestic Council (which controls national policy), and since Kissinger runs foreign policy, the House of Rockefeller already controls the government in everything but name. Having Nelson as Veep is a gun perpetually cocked at Ford's temple. If Jerry for some reason does not want to go along, a Secret Service man may look the other way while an assassin does a number on the President.

Let us assume that public revulsion at Rocky is so great that he is dumped from the Republican ticket. And let us assume also that Humphrey or another Democrat wins the Presidency. Does that mean that the royal Rockefellers would be stripped of their power? No, not unless the whole CFR socialist-fascist-world government strategy is repudiated. If Rocky is ousted, it will be a huge blow to his inflated ego and might set the Rockefeller Great Merger timetable back somewhat. The House of Rockefeller would simply be back to operating through the CFR. But their plan for world conquest will roll on unabated.

You see, we have the Rockepubs and the Rockedems, but there is not a dime's worth of difference. Both parties belong to the House of Rockefeller.

Epilogue

Now you have read the most important contents in *The Rockefeller File*. The assembled evidence is almost overwhelming, isn't it? And yet we have left out reams of important material.

This book was originally targeted for 144 pages. But we wound up with over 260 pages—even after omitting a great deal of explosive material. In order to keep the cost from climbing through the ceiling, we settled for the size you are reading. If we have not convinced you of the dangerous power of the House of Rockefeller in 200 pages, you probably would not believe another 200 pages anyway.

We deeply regret not using the voluminous files of research, all on very important subjects, which were gathered for this book. Several volumes could be written on Rockefeller efforts to involve America in World War I, World War II, Korea and Vietnam—and the profits they made from those conflicts. The alliance between Nazi Germany and the Rockefellers is truly shocking. (Hitler's Luftwaffe ran on Standard petrol, and the Rockefellers were partners in I. G. Farben Industries, whose thousands of war products included the poison gas used in Nazi death camps.) The no-win war in Vietnam was almost totally engineered, from its foolish beginning to its disastrous conclusion, by CFR minions.

Nothing has been said about Nelson's tenure as Governor of New York. We did not relate how he quadrupled state spending; we did not cover his campaign promises not to raise taxes—which were always followed by increases after he was elected. Neither have we touched upon Rocky's edifice complex, such as the $1.5 billion Albany Mall or his creation of "moral obligation bonds" to finance projects the voters had rejected.

Lack of space prevents us from discussing the Rockefeller power-play behind the myriad regional government
plans, which would abolish city, county and state lines—
thus destroying traditional local government and putting
the citizens at the mercy of unelected (and unremovable)
federal bureaucrats. The Family is also the prime mover
behind the push for "land use" controls which would
allow the government to dictate to you what you can or
cannot do with your own property.

But all of these stories will have to wait for another
book. We can summarize all of those bulging files of
research material by saying that the *Rockefellers want
federal control of everything*. Since they intend to control
the federal government, either directly or from behind the
scenes, this means that *they* will control every*thing*. And
when they control every*thing*, they will control
every*body*.

We have shown that the House of Rockefeller is worth
billions of dollars—and has considerable leverage over
hundreds of billions more, through influence over
the mega-banks, financial institutions, manufacturing and
petroleum production. The Family has used foundations
to preserve and multiply their wealth, and to mold public
opinion through education, the media and religion.
Through their Council on Foreign Relations they have
extended their influence in government, the Federal
Reserve, communications and education. An unquenched,
ruthless, psychopathic lust for monopolistic power has
motivated three generations of Rockefellers. Because
America is a large, diverse and decentralized nation, it has
taken them a hundred years to complete the scaffold
which would strangle freedom. Now they are ready to put
the rope around our necks and trip the lever.

The question is: Can we cut the rope before the Rockefellers drop the trap door? The most honest and realistic
answer is: Perhaps.

Let's not kid ourselves; resisting the power arrayed
against us won't be easy. Many persons who have read
this far won't even try—they will decide that it is hopeless

and simply return to their business interests or their bridge games. Others might decide that their best course is to support the House of Rockefeller! Switching sides and joining with your oppressors is as old as war. But if you haven't already been tapped, you are probably too late. The House of Rockefeller doesn't need you. (Sorry, Charlie!)

Unfortunately, some newly awakened patriots will go off on wild, impractical schemes. They may want to haul the Rockefellers before the courts in an attempt to put them in jail for their crimes and strip them of their power. But, let's face it, this is not going to happen. And such ill-conceived crusades end up hurting the cause of freedom far more than they help. There is, however, an Achilles heel in the Rockefeller plan for world dictatorship. It is that a Rockefeller triumph depends on their continued control of the U.S. government. If their influence in the federal government were removed, all of their Hitlerian dreams for world conquest would collapse. (Not that Nelson and David would spend the rest of their lives in rags, but at least you wouldn't either.)

Rockefeller control over the Executive branch of our government is deeply entrenched. The voters, for example, cannot fire the State Department bureaucracy. But there is a solution.

If a buzz saw suddenly went berserk and was ripping your house to pieces, what would you do? You would pull the plug, of course. The same thing must be done to the Rockefeller conspirators. The way to pull the plug on them is to gain control of the House of Representatives. All government spending bills must originate in the House. And Congress could refuse to pass any law pushing us further into World Government. We need 225 Congressmen who have the guts to say NO to the Rockefellers.

The Rockefellers can control key bureaucrats; they can buy and intimidate too many Senators. But a member of the House with enough character and enough support can remain independent of the Rockefeller Family.

The problem is that too many citizens listen to what a candidate says during the campaign, and then promptly forget about the issues—and what he does about them—after the election. A Congressman may go to Washington with good intentions, but succumb to the Rockefellers' siren song after he gets there. The pressures are tremendous. He is told that in order to get along, he must go along. If he goes along, his district gets fat government grants and contracts. If he doesn't go along, a Rockefeller-supported demagogue may defeat him in the next election.

What we must have is a "Truth In Advertising" standard for politicians. If you buy a product to do a specific job you expect it to do that job. Why should you expect less from elected politicians? We believe it is time to end the "vote and hope" system of elections, where you *hope* the new Congressman votes in the interest of his country after he gets to Washington. The usual result is that the constituency gets sold down the river. (A prime example is the confirmation of Nelson Rockefeller for the Vice Presidency when Congressional mail ran 24 to 1 against approval.)

We think any candidate worth supporting should sign an elementary contract *before* you agree to contribute to his campaign or otherwise support him. '76 PRESS has prepared such a contract, a copy of which appears on the next page.

Any political candidate who will hem, haw, double-talk or waffle in an effort to weasel out of signing such a "Truth In Politics" contract will surely not stand up to the blandishments of the Rockefellers once he is elected. Forget him. Be especially leery of the smiling, glad-handing, all-things-to-all-people moderate type of candidate. Such a "middle of the roader" will often compromise on the key issues and still manage to get re-elected time and time again. He is the most dangerous of all politicians.

The diabolical designs of the Rockefellers—their push for fascism-socialism at home and an international World Government—must become the key issue of the next

CANDIDATE'S CONTRACT©
Campaign Pledge

In the belief that "Truth In Advertising" should apply to politicians as well as to commercial products and services, I wholeheartedly agree that the citizenry is entitled to expect a candidate to keep his campaign promises once he is elected.

Therefore, as a candidate for election to the office of _____, I do hereby pledge, if elected, to adhere faithfully to the following positions on all votes and debates on these matters:

1. **I agree** to oppose any treaties, legislation, or other measures which would strengthen any regional or world bodies at the expense of American sovereignty.

2. **I agree** to oppose any proposals which would grant foreign aid, taxpayer-financed loans or loan guarantees, or other assistance to any Communist nation, whether such aid is given through national or international agencies.

3. **I agree** that the United States must retain military superiority over any potential aggressor; I will oppose any disarmament proposals that would support a World Government military force or that would not provide for thorough and reliable inspections of other nations.

4. **I agree** to oppose any deficit spending by the federal government, since such deficits increase the national debt and the inflation of our currency.

5. **I agree** that the expansion of government over every facet of our lives must be stopped, and that the marriage of Big Government and Big Business must be ended. I pledge to work to reduce the size and number of federal bureaucracies and agencies, not expand them.

Should I violate any of the promises made in this Campaign Pledge, I agree that the voters would be entitled to request my resignation from office.

_____
date

_____
witnessed by

_____
signed

Copies of this **Candidate's Contract**, printed in two colors on full-sized, parchment-like paper, may be ordered from the publisher. Send one dollar for every five copies ordered, plus a large (#10), stamped, self-addressed envelope, to '76 Press, P.O. Box 2686, Seal Beach, California 90740. ©1976 by '76 Press.

Congressional election. Any candidate who is too timid to criticize the House of Rockefeller in his campaign will not be strong enough to defend you against the Rockefellers when he gets to Washington.

The Rockefellers know that the House of Representatives is their Achilles heel. That is why they had their Common Cause lead the battle for the so-called Campaign Reform Act of 1974.

You can, however, turn the tables on the Rockefellers. Campaign spending laws will limit the use of this book by your candidate during his campaign. This does not prevent you from forming a committee to mass distribute the book in his area before the election. Such an end-run around the stacked *Insider* line is the only way for the American people to wrench control of Congress away from the House of Rockefeller.

In the past, whenever America was in great danger, her citizens risked their lives and rallied to the colors. But the battles were much simpler when the enemy wore a uniform instead of a Brooks Brothers suit, and spoke a foreign language instead of impeccable Ivy League English. Yesterday, the enemies of freedom used guns and bombs instead of bribery and flattery. They controlled the sea lanes instead of the air waves. Soldiers fought in foxholes instead of board rooms and at the ballot box.

Yes, it was all a lot less complicated then. But the war today is no less real and no less dangerous. Resistance to the Rockefellers' New World Order requires the same dedication and effort to win that it took to destroy Hitler. Fortunately, it does not require the sacrifices in blood which other wars have cost—that is, if the time, money and effort are expended *now*, before the only resistance possible is from behind barbed wire.

This book was not written simply to entertain you, merely to inform you, or even to frighten you. It was intended to be a razor-sharp sword which can sever the hangman's rope before it strangles us. We have published it. Now the rest is up to you. If you do nothing with this knowledge, the Rock will get a piece of you.

READ ABOUT THE GREATEST WHODUNIT OF ALL TIME:
THE COMMUNIST — SUPER-CAPITALIST CONSPIRACY

The following books will tell you the who, what, when, where, how, and why of the mystery that has perplexed millions of persons: why the super-rich have cooperated with international Communism, and what both sides hope to accomplish.

This list does not include every book that has been written on this crucial subject. It does include the titles I personally have found to be most helpful. I believe they are must reading for every person who wants to be informed on what is really happening in the world today.

Gary Allen

NATIONAL SUICIDE: MILITARY AID TO THE SOVIET UNION, by Antony C. Sutton. If America had an honest press, the contents of this book would have made page one news in every paper in the country. What could be more sensational than documented proof that the Soviet Union's military-industrial complex was created by the West, primarily by the United States? Written while the author was a Research Fellow at the prestigious Hoover Institute for War, Revolution and Peace at Stanford University, the thesis of *National Suicide* was never refuted or even answered by the Establishment. It was completely ignored. (Hardbound, 283 pages, $8.95)

KISSINGER ON THE COUCH, by Phyllis Schlafly and Admiral Chester Ward. A definitive analysis, both psychological and strategic, of the man who wields near-total control over U.S. foreign and defense policy: how he sprang to power from bases in the international and scientific elites; how he became the principal force in SALT disarmament agreements that have relegated the United States to second place in nuclear weapons; and how Kissinger has consistently deceived Congress and the American people. (Hardbound, 846 pages, $12.95)

NONE DARE CALL IT CONSPIRACY, by Gary Allen. This book, written as a primer on the Great Conspiracy, has sold four million copies in paperback. It presents a much broader view of *Insider* manipulations in finance and government than *The Rockefeller File.* The hardbound edition contains much material not found in the paperbound version, including a list of members and directors of the Council on Foreign Relations; participants in the Bilderberg Group; an annotated bibliography; and a complete index. (Hardbound, 190 pages, $5.95. Also available in German and Spanish)

WALL STREET AND THE BOLSHEVIK REVOLUTION, by Antony C. Sutton. His previous book, *National Suicide*, proved that the Soviet war machine was provided by the West. In this book, Professor Sutton uses government documents going back over fifty years to establish that this was no accident, but a deliberate policy since the days of the Bolshevik Revolution—when powerful and wealthy Americans bankrolled the establishment of the first Communist state. (Hardbound, 228 pages, $7.95)

WALL STREET AND F.D.R., by Antony C. Sutton. The myth-makers and rewriters of history have led generations of Americans to believe that Franklin Delano Roosevelt, a scion of the Establishment, was a "traitor to his class" because of his anti-wealth programs. Professor Sutton proves that precisely the opposite is true: FDR was put in power by the super-rich, who actually designed his "New Deal" to promote a fascist-socialist government that would eliminate their competition. (Hardbound, 200 pages, $7.95)

RICHARD NIXON: THE MAN BEHIND THE MASK, by Gary Allen. The man is gone, but the Establishment which made Nixon—and then broke him—remains in power. Every voter should read this book to understand how the grass roots is betrayed by socialist-fascist political manipulators operating behind the scenes. (Paperbound, 364 pages, $2.00)

THE NAKED CAPITALIST, by W. Cleon Skousen. For the first time, a highly placed socialist, Professor Carroll Quigley of Georgetown University, has admitted the existence of a conspiracy among the super-rich. Quigley wrote a 1500-page book documenting this "capitalist" plot to create a collectivist dictatorship in America. In this review of Quigley's book, *Tragedy And Hope*, Skousen cites the amazing proof Quigley has assembled. (Paperbound, 130 pages, $2.00)

WORLD WITHOUT CANCER: THE STORY OF VITAMIN B17, by G. Edward Griffin. We are not qualified to comment on the medical accuracy of this two-volume set, which contends that cancer is a deficiency disease like scurvy or pellagra that can be prevented. But the evidence assembled here, to prove that a Rockefeller-controlled drug cartel has subverted science to protect entrenched political interests, is shocking and convincingly presented. (Paperbound, 592 pages, $4.00)

If any of these books are not available at your local bookstore, they may be ordered from '76 PRESS. See the order blank at the back of this book.

After reading this book, you will never look at national and world events in the same way again.

Over four million copies of this explosive best seller have been distributed since it first appeared three years ago. It became one of the most widely read books in the country— without the benefit of a single review, advertisement, or promotion in the mass media.

The reason for its phenomenal success is that for the first time, someone had stated—and assembled the facts to prove —that conspiratorial forces behind the scenes actually control our government and dictate its policies. Read it and judge it for yourself!

1 copy — $1.00	25 copies — $10.00
3 copies — $2.00	100 copies — $30.00
10 copies — $5.00	1,000 copies — $250.00

Use order blank on the last page

Order Form

Please send me the following books:

Quantity	Title	Price	Total
————	National Suicide	$ 8.95	————
————	Kissinger on the Couch	12.95	————
————	None Dare Call It Con- spiracy, *hardbound*	5.95	————
————	None Dare Call It Con- spiracy, *German*	5.75	————
————	None Dare Call It Con- spiracy, *Spanish*	3.00	————
————	Wall Street and the Bolshevik Revolution	7.95	————
————	Wall Street And F.D.R.	7.95	————
————	Richard Nixon: The Man Behind The Mask	2.00	————
————	The Naked Capitalist	2.00	————
————	World Without Cancer	4.00	————

TOTAL $————

Please complete the shipping information on the back of this coupon, add $ .75 per book ordered for postage and handling, and include payment in full for your order.